PREPARING FOR BREXIT

HOW TO SURVIVE THE FOOD SHORTAGES

CONTENTS

Introduction

Introduction

This book is for anyone who is concerned about possible shortages of food and other supplies following Brexit on 29th March 2019, or whichever date is decided by Parliament.

This book will go through the reasons why it may be sensible to give some forethought and preparation in case of shortages after Brexit.

The sections on where to start, what might be sensible to stockpile, where to get it and how to store it will guide readers in how to prepare for future shortages in food and other supplies. The book will help readers identify what they require and help them to devise a plan that meets the needs of them and their family.

There is also information on stretching your supplies out to last longer if needed, sample meal plans and shopping lists and alternative food sources to consider if it comes to it.

These are uncertain times and preparing for future shortages now will give huge peace of mind to those who are concerned about the future.

Although the book is largely concerned about making preparations before Brexit, it also contains information which will be useful post Brexit should food shortages become an issue.

1 – Why Are People Worried About Food Shortages After Brexit?

Regardless of how you feel about the Referendum and other events leading up to Brexit, it is hard to ignore the reports of possible food shortages after Brexit takes place. Nearly every day, there are more stories in the media about problems which will befall the UK following Brexit. Detailed reasons are given below, but in summary many people feel that there is too much of a risk of food shortages or significant price rises occurring in the next few months and wish to ensure that they can survive these by having food stockpiled.

Many of the reasons people are stockpiling food are related to the possibility of a No Deal Brexit (at the time of publication for this book) but even if this is resolved, there are still other reasons why food and other resources are likely to be in shorter supply or more expensive in 2019.

The UK imports large amounts of food

This is a fact that can't be argued with. More fresh food, vegetables, meat and other products are imported than are grown here, with 30% of imported food coming from Europe.

Even if farmers started now, it would not be possible for the produce that is imported to be grown in the UK. A 2017 report (Benton et. al) concluded that although it would be sensible for the UK to diversify what it does produce, it cannot replace everything that is imported.

A No Deal Brexit would instantly mean that what is imported from Europe would no longer be able to get into the country as quickly due to increased checks and bureaucracy. For fresh food that is currently picked one day in Europe and in the supermarket three days later, it will not last the increased transit time so will go off and not reach the shops in time so would not be available.

The huge uncertainty around Brexit means it is hard to predict the consequences of any deal that is made, other than the author's opinion that it isn't going to make importing food any easier. The likelihood is that prices will increase and potentially there will still be problems in getting food imported and onto shelves.

Fragile supply chains
The food industry has very fragile supply chains. They work on a three day system in terms of getting food into shops and onto shelves.

The recent news that the Government had suggested the food industry stockpile food to guard against post Brexit shortages confirms the fragility of food supplies to the UK. The food industry states it does not have storage facilities for more food so they do not have the capacity to stockpile food.

The very fact that the Government suggested this as something that should be done has made many more people consider stockpiling for themselves before Brexit happens.

Technical Notes

At the time of writing the first edition of this book, the Government is in the process of issuing a selection of "Technical Notes" to inform and guide the UK population on what may happen if No Deal Brexit occurs and what can be done to prepare.

Many people believe that there may be one for the public to stockpile food, although as yet there hasn't been. The technical notes that have already been issued have generally given worrying information such as the increased cost of credit cards and there is a climate of apprehension on what information may be conveyed by future technical notes.

As subsequent batches of technical notes are published, with their contents arguably becoming more worrying each time, the lack so far of any related to personal or national food supplies is causing concern amongst many that these are yet to come, therefore their contents are likely to be more worrying than what has been published already.

Many people are trying to start their stockpiles before all of the technical notices are issued as they fear that should a food stockpiling one be produced it will cause panic and food shortages due to the general public panic buying.

Update: At the time of writing the second edition of this book (March 2019)- there still has not been any information published by the Government to help people manage their personal food supplies and we are three days from the original Exit date of 29th March.

Loss of ability to produce UK food

The UK food industry is heavily reliant on workers from abroad. The fruit industry is already suffering hugely as thousands of European workers who normally help harvest fruit such as raspberries have not come to work this year due to the uncertainties around Brexit and Europe. There have been many news articles stating that farmers around the country have been unable to harvest their crops. So even if it is grown here, without the labour to harvest it, it will not make it into the shops for people to purchase.

The meat industry is also hugely reliant on foreign workers. Animals produced for meat such as cattle, sheep and pigs need to be killed in an abattoir in order to be sold to the public. It is a legal requirement that abattoirs have their own vets in attendance for animal welfare purposes and to ensure that procedures are followed correctly.

It is less widely known that over 90% of abattoir vets are from Europe and other countries. If the vets choose to or have to leave it will mean that the abattoirs will not be able to kill and process meat for food production which would lead to a huge shortage of meat, particularly if combined with a reduction in the availability of meat from Europe at the same time.

As has been seen with the fruit and vegetable industry, many European and other workers are choosing either not to come to the UK, or if already living here to leave. If this continues into other areas of food production, particularly the meat industry then food shortages and price increases look very likely.

Exceptional weather

The exceptional hot summer of 2018 has given great difficulties to farmers. Price increases up to 45% are already predicted for plants such as carrots and peas due to the freak weather of 2018. Although these increases can take 18 months to filter through to the supermarket shelves, they are on the way.

The hot weather has also caused problems for livestock farmers as it has hampered wheat and other livestock food production. Many farmers are having to use food they would normally save for winter time to feed stock now and many are slaughtering stock early to reduce the number of animals they are having to feed. This is causing a crisis in the farming industry which will continue to unfold.

This will cause price increases as food is having to be bought in to feed stock, as well as reduced availability in the longer term as herd sizes have been reduced early so less stock will be sent into the food chain when it was planned to be, so decreasing supplies which will increase the cost of meat. If farmers need to import animal feed this will create further problems in terms of how they can source feed and the costs involved if it is possible to do so. This means it is almost certain that meat prices will rise significantly over the next few months.

Increased feed prices will also eventually have a knock on effect on the price of milk and dairy products as the cattle used to produce them also need feeding so if the costs to produce them rise then so will the retail prices.

The perfect storm of Brexit and associated uncertainties and problems combined with the consequences of freak weather mean some degree of food shortages or price rises are likely to occur in the next few months to coincide with Brexit. At the time of writing, there is already an increasing feeling from many people that prices are already beginning to increase significantly over a range of products. The number of articles in the news about how prices of different products are likely to increase adds to the uncertainty and unease felt by many people about food supplies and prices in the future.

Many people who believe that prices will, or have already started to rise due to Brexit and other factors have decided to take matters into their own hands in terms of ensuring that they have sufficient food and other resources available as they do not necessarily believe that the UK Authorities have the capability or capacity to provide this for the entire population-either at all or at an affordable price.

Many people would rather have the peace of mind of knowing that they have resources stored away in case they are needed rather than the worry of seeing how events unfold over the next few months and being dependent on the Government and other agencies to ensure that sufficient food is available to the general population.

Just in the last few weeks, it has been announced that the Government has created a new Ministerial Post- Food Supplies Minister. This may be reassuring to some as it suggests that the Government is looking at this problem. But for many, this has increased concerns as they feel it shows that this is going to be a real problem, or why create a new Ministerial Brief for the issue. It is worth noting that the last time the UK had a minister with a similar role, the country had rationing. Hopefully not a sign of things to come but this is how many people are seeing this and are increasing their stockpiling efforts accordingly.

Whether people believe that there will be total food shortages or just shortages of some items with increased food prices varies, but many people feel that having some resources stashed away "just in case" gives them valuable peace of mind in terms of the future for them and their families.

Forward Purchasing vs Panic Buying

There have been many stories in the media recently about large organisations stocking up with supplies that are intended to last them into the projected Brexit period. They have done this to guard against the effects of a No Deal Brexit. Many large food retailers and manufacturers are doing this as well as organisations as the Army. The Army came up with the novel phrase "Forward Purchasing". This is a great phrase for anyone wanting to start their own stockpile to guard against the consequences of Brexit.

Forward Purchasing is basically prepping- ensuring that you have supplies that you will need for a period going into the future. With the current chaotic political system, this seems to be a sensible approach and if the large organisations are doing it, then it seems logical that individuals may wish to do this too rather than relying on the Government to organise it.

There has been a bit of a backlash in the media recently against preppers. Some people have the view that the preppers will be the cause of any shortages that may occur. This is the wrong way round- preppers if anything will help the situation should food shortages happen as they will be the ones who have supplies already and won't be fighting it out in the supermarket for the last loaf of bread. Preppers will have purchased their supplies before any shortages occurred, at a time when the supermarkets were easily able to replenish their stocks to replace what the preppers purchased for their stockpiles so will have been replaced.

Shortages are likely to be exacerbated by the panic buyers. Panic buying will be what happens if non preppers become worried about potential or actual food shortages and try to buy as much as they can in one go. This is what will cause fights in the supermarkets and shortages as people grab whatever they can carry. The preppers will be in the position where they know they have everything they need and don't have to risk a potentially dangerous trip to a supermarket full of panic buyers. This will be beneficial to those who haven't prepped as that will mean fewer people in the supermarket trying to purchase food at the same time, so there will be more food available for the people who need it as the preppers will have theirs already.

2- Prepping: What Is It and Why Do It?

What is it?
In short, "making preparations for a future emergency that may or may not occur". The word Prepper comes from Preparing. People who do Prepping tend to be known as Preppers.

Many people when thinking of Preppers or Prepping may envisage survivalists planning for the apocalypse with massive stores of food and weapons; living in the middle of nowhere waiting for whatever disaster they think will occur. Whilst this is certainly the stereotypical image of Preppers and Prepping, it is a very extreme version.

- Have you ever put money aside for an unexpected bill?
- Have you ever put a bit of extra food away in case of bad weather stopping you getting to the shop?
- Have you ever bought candles and stored them in case of a power cut?
- Have you ever kept wellies and a spare jumper in your car in winter in case you got stuck in the snow?

All of these examples are also prepping, just on a much smaller scale. Each of these is making a preparation for a bad event that may or may not happen but if it does the preparation will make it much easier to deal with. If you have done any of these examples or similar than you have already dipped a toe into the world of prepping.

There are increasing numbers of people in the UK who are quietly building stockpiles of food and supplies in case of emergency. Many have done it for years but their numbers are increasing dramatically as Brexit approaches and prepping becomes something that more people think about doing due to their concerns about the future.

Why Do it?

People prep for future events and emergencies so that if the emergency occurs it will be easier to deal with and get through than if the preparations hadn't been made.

What do People Prep For?

People prep for all sorts of reasons and possible scenarios. As well as the apocalypse on the far end of the scale, there are plenty of other things that can happen where it would be very handy to have some spare food or resources available. Many of the following scenarios have happened in the UK in the last few years:

- Flooding – in some cases enough to cut areas off for days and weeks
- Power cuts – can last for days
- Snow – particularly last winter can either stop you being able to get out to the shops or cut the shops off from deliveries so even if you can get there they have nothing to buy
- Extreme weather e.g. storms- can cause flooding / power cuts / inability for food to be delivered to shops or your ability to go shopping

Other things that could happen to disrupt your ability to be able to purchase food when needed could include:

- Illness — if you are too poorly to leave the house then you won't be able to go shopping. Internet shopping and takeaways are great but many people live in areas where these don't deliver and they may not (especially takeaways) be a sustainable option.
- Unexpected bill- a huge bill for the car or a house repair if you have no savings or stored food means you are likely to struggle to pay it and maintain your usual shopping habits.
- Loss of earnings — losing hours at work or losing your job. You could go from having enough to get by to being unable to afford food once your other expenses are paid.
- Rapid inflation in price rises making many food items unaffordable on your current wages or budget.
- Food shortages- food just not being in the shops to purchase.

The above scenarios are everyday events and in each of them, having a few supplies stashed away could make life much easier. Some people have a couple of months' worth of food stored so they would know they can eat if an emergency occurred- giving one less worry whilst they deal with their emergency.

Other people may only have a few bits stashed away but even that will help, whether it tides them over for a few days or if they buy a few bits of food but supplement what they can buy with supplies they had stored away to reduce their costs for a while.

Whether people choose to have a few bits stashed away just in case so they know they are fine for a couple of days or so, or whether they decide to have a couple of months' worth of everything they might need is up to them.

Choosing what sort of prepping you might want to do is covered further along in the book but something is better than nothing so any prepping even a few spare tins could be something you were very glad you did if an incident occurred in the future.

Government Guidelines
Interestingly, it is very hard to find specific Government advice on the amount of food households should have stored for emergencies. Current publications produced by the Government (e.g. What To Do Before, During and After A Flood- published by the Environment Agency) advise keeping "bottled water and non-perishable foods" as part of the emergency flood plan that vulnerable households should make in case they are involved in a flood.

Previous Government publications give slightly more detail. "Preparing yourself, your family and your community for emergencies" (National Risk Register 2010) advises that individuals gather essential supplies including tinned food and bottled water for use if an emergency occurs.

"Preparing for Emergencies- What You Need to Know" (2004) advises people that it is "always useful to have bottled water, ready-to-eat (tinned) food with an opener in case you have to remain in your home for several days" if an emergency happens.

Governments in the UK issued advice within public information booklets which included the idea of holding a store of tinned food in case of emergency. The fact that it is hard to find current guidance does not mean that it is no longer a good idea to do so.

Amazingly, as recently as 1991, there was a network of Government owned and maintained food stockpiles around the country. It is fascinating that until relatively recently there was a National Stockpile of food that could be utilized in a national emergency. The stockpile was disposed of in 1991 and so a national resource was lost. It seems like a very different era in terms of planning for emergencies. Many people who are planning to stockpile food for post Brexit will remember these times. As the Government no longer has the capacity to implement or run a National Stockpile, it is easy to see why so many people feel they would rather take matters into their own hands by setting up their own stockpile than hoping that it won't be necessary in a few months' time.

Other countries, including Sweden and the USA advise citizens keep their own supplies. Within the UK, agencies such as the Police and the Red Cross have personal emergency planning information which includes the advice that people should keep some tinned / non-perishable food and supplies in case there is an emergency.

As we have been advised to keep some emergency supplies by our Government for years and this is still done so by other countries around the world it seems sensible to keep some supplies in just in case.

Prepping- Possible Outcomes

If you decide to prep and then there isn't an emergency, in this instance Brexit doesn't cause shortages and price rises as many people currently believe what will the outcome be? If you've prepped sensibly then:
- You have a store of supplies stashed away for other emergencies which is good for peace of mind.
- You can rotate the stocks through your day to day eating so won't be left with a stock of food you'll end up throwing out so you haven't wasted money
- You will have however extra food available that you can eat so saving money at the point you decide you no longer need to keep it by eating it -giving a cheap month as you will have to buy far less food. If you've put some cash aside too then even better you can treat yourself.
- You could decide to save some of your store just in case and use the rest- peace of mind and a few meals you've already paid for. In the meantime your stores have given you valuable peace of mind about the future.

So worst case scenario for your prepping if it's not needed for Brexit- you save some money by eating your stores. Best case scenario if it is needed then you'll be very glad you had it. Both outcomes show that prepping hasn't been a waste of money and has given valuable peace of mind.

Prepping can be done to the level that suits you- anything between a few tins and storing supplies to last weeks or months. Either way if done sensibly, the supplies won't be wasted and will come in handy either in case of emergency when they are needed or by saving a lot of money when you decide it's safe to use them all.

So if you wish to prep, it is difficult to find reasons not to but plenty of reasons why you should.

3- How Prepared Do You Want To Be?

Any prepping is better than no prepping if an event happens to make the supplies needed. Everyone will have different ideas on how many supplies they feel they need to be adequately prepared in the event of an emergency.

Different levels of prepping with key information on them are shown below:

Emergency box / cupboard
- Enough for the household for 2-3 days.
- Has sufficient food and water for everyone but may not have supplies that you would want if an incident continued longer than 2-3 days.
- Ideal for if you're ill and can't get out for a couple of days, or if bad weather means the local shops are either inaccessible or empty for a couple of days until deliveries arrive again.
- Easy to set up and maintain as likely to be in one box / cupboard.
- Easy to buy everything you need quickly.
- Great way to start prepping and some people will be content to have this level of preparedness just in case without going any further.

A Weeks' Worth

- Not just a double of the Emergency box above!
- For a weeks' supplies you would want to think about supplies you could live without for 3 days but wouldn't want to be without for a week such as toiletries / toothpaste in case what you had ran out during that week (you could probably do without or squeeze an extra days' worth out of what you were using for a short 2-3 day incident) so non-food supplies and medication would also become part of your planning.
- You would want to consider more variety in terms of the food and supplies you were storing. For 2-3 days, the novelty value would be high but beyond that people are going to want to eat more than one or two different types of meal if possible (although something is better than nothing in a survival situation).
- Still likely to be a small enough amount to easily store in a cupboard (unless you are prepping for a large number of people)

A Fortnight

- As before when moving up to a week's supplies- not just a matter of doubling everything. Variety is becoming more important.
- Likely to be becoming harder to store so you would need to start to think about where to put it all and consider beginning an inventory / meal plan if you haven't already to monitor what you have and what you still need to achieve your prepping goal.

- A fortnight is a long time! If possible, it is advisable to include some treats to have in the time to improve morale. These could include things like chocolate (bars, biscuits, spread) or long life biscuits and cakes.
- Depending on how many you are prepping for, it is going to get more difficult to build the stockpile at a fortnights' worth of supplies and beyond.

A Month and Beyond

- This goes to a new level of prepping. Just as before, variety is going to be very important but while we can survive well enough for a couple of weeks on a reasonably varied diet beyond that you will need to give more thought to ensuring nutritional needs are properly met so would want to try to achieve a balanced diet with the resources available (i.e. what you put away).
- However well you plan your stock, vitamins are an excellent addition to help ensure everyone you are prepping for keeps healthy. Vitamins can be bought cheaply and have a long life so can be bought early on in the process if you are planning to do a lot of stockpiling.
- You will definitely need to be putting thought into how to store your supplies by now. Inventories and planning are advisable too so that you keep track of what you have.
- As storage requirements become an issue, you should look at adding foods that take less space but keep well and deliver high calorific value to keep everyone going. These would include larger quantities of dried lentils, oats and rice. Pasta is good too but rice is far more space efficient.

- If you end up having to rely on your stocks to survive then better to have boring pasta and lentils to keep you going amongst some tins then not. With smaller stocks (so for shorter time periods) you could probably mostly live on tinned foods but for the longer term you will need to increase the proportion of these dried foods. They are also a cheap and easy way to add capacity to your store and how long it will last. Make sure your supplies include lots of herbs and spices to make the foods more interesting.
- Just as increasing the proportion of dried foods becomes more necessary the longer you intend your stores to sustain you, so does the importance of maintaining morale. Make sure you include some treats in your store to help with this.

Not Full Prepping But Stockpiling Things That May Become Expensive or Hard to Get Hold Of

- Very Brexit specific prepping here!
- Identify what items you think will be hard or impossible to get hold of should Brexit turn out badly- whether they just won't be available or whether they will become very expensive.
- Obvious and long life (and therefore worth stock piling if you use them) examples include:
  - Olive oil
  - Pasta
  - Tinned Tomatoes
  - Tomato puree
  - Dried herbs and spices
  - Garlic (granules / pastes and bulbs)

- o Preserved veg / fruit e.g. artichokes, jarred peppers, olives
- o European Wines
- o Pesto
- o Luxury brands / spreads such as Nutella or Biscoff spread

- Perishable food items which are likely to become less available / more expensive:
  - o Fresh fruit
  - o Fresh veg such as tomatoes, courgettes, lettuces
  - o Fresh potatoes
  - o Cheese (as well as the French and Italian cheeses that will spring to mind, 50% of Cheddar is imported so that is also likely to become more expensive or hard to get).
- Look through your kitchen cupboards at where foods you eat come from and see which come from Europe. Potentially any or all of those could also be at risk.
- Make a list of the foods you wouldn't want to be without and that will form a large part of your planning. It is good to identify the perishable foods too so that you can be considering if there is anything you can do to set up an alternative source if they can no longer be imported or become too expensive.
- This sort of prepping is for people who are doubtful that full food shortages will happen but don't want to take the chance of foods they eat now that come from Europe becoming unavailable or unaffordable so are stocking up on them now.

4- Where to Start

Everyone should start with the Emergency Box / Store for 2-3 days' worth of supplies even if they plan to build larger stockpiles. Starting with this gives experience of planning, purchasing and storing a small stockpile which will be helpful for doing larger stockpiles later. Doing the first Emergency Store will give you a real sense of achievement that you have supplies to see your family through an emergency if needed as well as a better understanding of the processes involved in stockpiling food and the amount of storage you will need to find.

Determine who you are prepping for
Just you? You and your partner? You and your family? Pets?

Identifying who you are prepping for is vital as it means you can plan what supplies you need more accurately, obviously the more people you prep for the more supplies you need but also the more people you are prepping for, the more individual requirements in terms of dietary and other needs there will be to get your head round and plan for. Don't forget pets if you have them too.

Safety and Security
One of the most important things to understand before you start stockpiling is the need for secrecy. If food shortages happen, and people get hungry and desperate for food then they can do unpleasant things. You should not tell people that you are prepping. If people know you are stockpiling food and then food shortages strike, this will make you a target for firstly requests for help but then potentially theft as people try to secure food supplies for themselves.

Hard as it is, you need to identify who you are prepping for and work to that plan without telling people outside your close family that you are prepping for (and then only if they can be trusted not to tell others).

If you have already thought about or started prepping and have mentioned it to other people, consider how you might reduce risks. You could say you decided it wasn't worth doing, or that you couldn't afford it, or that you decided just a few tins were enough and have a small supply (say your Emergency Box) just in case anyone did come looking for supplies from you.

Continue prepping but keep the supplies hidden away so that if anyone did come it would be convincing that you just had your Emergency Box which if needed you could sacrifice in the knowledge that the real stockpile was safely hidden. This is a good reason to have stores hidden in different areas around the house although it does cause more work in terms of stock rotation, and generally remembering what you have and where it is.

If you are worried about friends and family that you aren't prepping for who aren't stockpiling, you could mention in general terms about the news and suggest they get a few tins in, but if they won't listen ultimately that is their choice. You have to focus on prepping for your own household. By all means get a few extra tins in if you think you might want to give them to friends or neighbours but consider how you would do this without alerting them to the fact that you have a stockpile which is keeping you and your family going and becoming a target for others.

What sort of Stockpile are you aiming for?

Consider the following when deciding how large a stockpile you are aiming for:

- How long would you like your supplies to last in an emergency or food shortage situation?

  If you are happy with building a stockpile to last a week that is fine and you don't need to worry about longer term planning (but can add to it later if you wish). If you want many weeks' or months' worth then this may influence your planning and purchasing from the start.

- How many are you prepping for?

  The more people you are prepping for, the larger your stockpile will need to be and the more it will cost to do.

- How much storage do you realistically have?

  Now you've done the Emergency Box, you will be better able to visualise the storage requirements of a larger stockpile.

- How much money are you able to put into creating your stockpile?

Some people are happy adding a couple of items a week with their normal shopping which makes the costs less noticeable. Other people will want to do a few large extra shopping trips which will be an additional expense. If you are prepping for Brexit, the closer it comes the less time you have to prep so the more likely it is that you will have to do a big shop and spend more money in less time to create your stockpile.

Once you have considered all these factors and looked at the size of stockpile you would like versus your available resources in terms of storage and finances, you will be better able to decide what level of stockpile it is realistic to aim for. If you get it done sooner than planned you can always keep adding to it. We all have different abilities and aspirations for prepping- do what is practical and appropriate for you and your family.

<u>Organising Your Supplies</u>
Once you have decided how large you want your store to be, you need to think about how to organise and use it in the most efficient way.

First In First Out
To reduce the risk of anything going out of date, it is best to use a First In First Out system. Whatever went into the store first gets used first therefore ensuring that the items with the longest shelf life are always in the store.

It is good to have this principle in mind before you begin buying and storing anything so that you can set things up to work in this way from the start rather than once you have bought a fair amount and having to take it all out to put back in a different order.

One way to do this that works if you have lots of the same item (such as tinned beans or tinned tomatoes) on a shelf is to always put the newest one at the back and pull the "older" ones out to the front. If you do this every time everything will be in the right order. It's easiest to do this if you have deep shelves that you can stack far back in. Always double check the Best Before date on the tins in case you have bought one with a shorter date than the ones you already have- if this happens just put it in the right place so that the ones with the longest date are at the back and the shortest are at the front.

If you are storing things in boxes or shallow shelves and are considering putting them in on their sides to maximise capacity, one trick is to write on the top of the tin the Best Before date and what it is. Then you will easily be able to pull out the item you want and make sure it is the oldest one.

More in the Cupboards
An extension of the First In First Out system. As part of your prepping, it is a good idea to increase what you have in your normal day to day cupboards. This reduces the risk that you will have to go into your stockpile for something on a normal day. Rather than buying something when you're about to or have run out of it, try to have the new one in the cupboard behind it if funds allow. This is an easy habit to get into and combining all the different day to day items in the kitchen probably add at least a couple more days' worth of food to your supplies if an emergency happens.

Stock Rotation

As you should be largely stockpiling things that your family eats anyway, you need to rotate your stockpiled food through your normal day to day living to make sure it is used before going out of date and avoiding the risk of ending up with 30 out of date tins of beans or whatever in a cupboard somewhere in your house when you've been buying and eating them as part of daily life.

When you decide you need to buy something you're running low on, put the item you just bought to the back of your stockpile. This way the stockpile has the item with the longest shelf life. Take the one at the front away and put that in your kitchen for day to day eating. This way nothing will get forgotten about and wasted. Even better, buy two of whatever it is, put them both at the back and take one out for the kitchen- increasing your stockpile as well as ensuring it has the longest lasting contents.

Organisation and Record Keeping

As your stores increase, it can become harder to remember what you've got. Record keeping helps in terms of knowing what you still need to get and also for planning meals from it should the need arise. Organising your stockpile will enable you to get maximum value in terms of money, space and usability from its contents. There are a few ways to organise your supplies. The simplest in some ways is pen and paper but this can become difficult to manage as the size of the stockpile increases.

There are a couple of specialist prepping journal notebooks available on Amazon which are both very good. "Prepping Planner" allows for a years' worth of prepping with progress records, meal planner and shopping list pages, meal information to see at a glance how many days' worth of supplies you have as well as blank inventories and a non-food essentials checklist. This is a comprehensive record book and will appeal to those who like to be highly organised and have all the information they need available at a glance.

The other one is "Food Stockpiling Journal"- this is much simpler with pages for different food types e.g. beans, meat, fish, pasta etc. for you to put your own lists in to work through as well as sections for meal ideas, items for family members and non-food items. Both are useful prepping tools but have very different styles in terms of the information you put in and have to hand.

Alternatively, if you prefer computers you could set up a spreadsheet. This can be set up however works best for you and should make it easy to identify how many of something you have and when they go out of date. One point to bear in mind before going down the computer route however is that if the power goes off, so does the computer unless it's a laptop but they need to be charged sufficiently. For this reason, if you are worried about power cuts proceed with caution with keeping your information electronically.

Storage

Have at least an idea of where you will put it all before you go shopping! Obviously the more you are going to buy in one go, the more important this is. If you're adding bits and bobs to your regular shop you can probably put those somewhere while you decide about your main storage. If you're planning on a huge shopping trip you will find it much easier to have a clear plan on where it is going to go once you get it home. Storage is discussed in detail later in the book.

Make a Plan

Make a shopping list of what you want to purchase before you go shopping. It is all too easy to get carried away but if you have a list to try to stick to you should come away with what you need to create enough meals and food easily for your family to live on for the size of stockpile you are shopping for. Making a meal plan and building your shopping list from there is a good way to plan your purchases. Suggested foods and meals are covered in more detail later in the book.

What to Buy

The short answer to this is – supplies that will let you survive without needing to go to the shops for however long you intend your stockpile to last. Either because you can't get to the shops, or because the shops haven't got any food to sell.

These supplies have three categories all of which have their own chapters later in the book.

Water
Food
Non-Food

In addition to these, there are also some items of equipment that whilst not necessarily essential could come in very useful which also have their own chapter.

5- What to Buy: Water

Why water before food?
Because we can survive longer without food than we can without water.

Why water when we are prepping for food shortages?
Because if we are prepping we may as well do it properly. If you're going to have a stockpile to help you get through emergency situations, it should be equipped get you through more than just the emergency of food shortages. Water shortages can happen for numerous reasons- broken pipes, flooding or contamination. We frequently hear of areas that have had their water cut off and are relying on bottled water. Many local authorities advise that people keep a few bottles of water in reserve in case of problems with tap water.

Of course, this book is about prepping for Brexit and all that goes with it. Everyone is worried about this causing food shortages but people are also concerned about power shortages due to the relationship the UK has with the EU in terms of exporting and importing electricity. If the relevant agreements are not concluded before Brexit, power shortages could become an issue. Nobody knows how these would manifest- whether as long term power cuts or intermittent black outs. Either way, electricity is needed to power the water supply and some houses require electricity to pump water from the water tanks and out of the taps. Enough reasons to think about stockpiling some water as well as food.

Recommendations on how much water to store range from 2-4 litres per person per day. This is a wide variation as the 2 litres is for drinking only (although some people usually have less, others will have more) and the 4 litres would be to include things like washing, cooking and toilet flushing.

In calculating how much you should store, consider how much you think each family member drinks in a day (including pets) and remembering that we get some of our fluid from food and other drinks so if you're planning to eat a lot of soup one day you may need to drink less water that day, or if you have dry food on a hot day you would need more. Breastfeeding women need a lot more.

Take into account your own situation- how much storage can you devote to storing water? Do you live near the sea or a river or stream that you could take water from to flush the toilet with? Would you feel happy using water purification tablets and filters if necessary to make water collected in water butts etc. drinkable?

For a single person, 2-2.5 litres a day would probably be sufficient for drinking and cooking if you were happy to collect the odd bottle from outside for toilet flushing etc. If you have a family you should work out how much you think each person would need to get your daily total. For a family of two adults and three children, 10 litres a day could be a reasonable figure if they had access to other water for flushing toilets if needed and saved water from tins (many tinned veg come in water) for cooking with. Three children would be unlikely to need as much water as three adults so some may be left over to give the adults slightly more.

Water takes up a lot of storage space! Make this easier by buying varying sizes of bottle to fit into different spaces- the packs of 500ml / 1 litre ones will fit well under beds or at the bottom of wardrobes. The 2 litre ones go well in a kitchen cupboard either standing or piled on their sides. They will also fit behind kitchen kickboards (make sure they aren't lying on concrete though- ensure the floor is clean and has old carpet on it if necessary). You could keep a few bottles in the freezer which will help keep it cold if the power goes off.

If you have a deep shelving unit you can hide away somewhere in the house, you can get a surprising amount in there but be sure to use the bottom shelf so the shelves can cope with the weight and don't become top heavy and at risk of toppling over.

It would be useful to get at least a couple of 5 litre bottles of water as this is a good size to use if you need to go out and collect some from a river or stream for toilet flushing water. If that situation happened, you would use a 5 litre bottle up first to give you the empty container to gather more water with from outside.

10 litres of water a day for a week is 70 litres. That amount is probably storable around the house if you are imaginative but more than this is going to get difficult. It is a good idea to invest in some water purification tablets- each tablet will treat a litre of water. You can also get special bottles which filter the water to make it drinkable. These aren't cheap at approximately £27 at time of writing for a bottle and additional filter that would do 260 litres, but the cost of that much water at 10p a litre comes to £26 which makes it seem a much better deal.

A combination of a few days' to a weeks' worth of actual water together with a good quality filtering bottle (and spare filter if you can stretch to it) and some water purification tablets will give a good 2 -3 weeks' worth of water which is enough to give some peace of mind in this area with a much reduced storage requirement. This does however assume you are confident that you can collect water from outside to filter or purify with the tablets.

However you decide to manage your water collection, it is best to start sooner rather than later to give you time to collect a reasonable amount. It's heavy so you may find getting a couple of bottles every time you go to the shops is easier in terms of carrying it all into the house than buying it all at once. Bottled water has a good shelf life, lasting at least a year. If possible store it in a dark place with stable temperature to increase the time it lasts.

6- What to Buy: Food

Obviously you will need food, but you need to make sure it is the right food- long lasting and mostly rotatable through your day to day eating. Your family will need to be happy to eat it and ensure you buy at least some ingredients that can make meals without too much work (if Brexit and food shortages hit badly enough for us to be living off our supplies we will have enough to worry about without spending hours cooking).

In terms of prioritising what to get first if stockpiling gradually, this could vary depending on your circumstances. Personally I started by buying everything needed for a couple of weeks' worth, then added significantly more bulk items (rice, pasta, lentils, water that could be survived on if absolutely necessary) and then buying a few weeks' worth of everything else to go with it. Once that block of supplies was complete I'd begin the process again to do another months' worth.

One thing to consider is that if you have a specific dietary issue such as needing gluten free food, look to buy large amounts of whatever specialist foods were needed to ensure your supplies were secured and then look to buying other things which are more easily obtainable. Anything that you or a member of your family cannot do without should be prioritised- another example would be baby formula if you had a young baby.

Suggestions for foods that are suitable for stockpiling as they come in tins, jars or are dried are detailed in the table below. This is not an exhaustive list but will give ideas to start you off.

Tailor your food planning to the dietary needs and preferences of you and your household. If you're all vegetarian then you won't be buying any meat products and will have more space for vegetarian items but the list is intended to show the range of foods that would be useful to have stored in order to give ideas of what you would need and want to have.

Whilst it is good to have a stockpile of versatile ingredients that can be used for lots of different meals, it is helpful to have at least some meals planned (so you list the meals you want and buy the ingredients you need) so that you know you can definitely make a certain number of meals even if you are happy to "rustle up" other meals with the ingredients you have. This will also make your shopping more efficient as you will know you're buying however many meals (and therefore days' worth) in each shop. When meal planning, try to strike a balance between the family favourites (for familiarity and comfort food in challenging times) and ensuring a varied diet with a selection of different meals.

Foods are put into different categories to make it clearer and easier to identify foods in the same or different categories from each other:

Food Category	Foods
Pulses	Dried lentils, chickpeas (especially if you like hummus), soup mix, beans. Tinned chickpeas, baked beans, borlotti beans, kidney beans, cannellini beans etc. Tinned lentils.
Pasta	Dried spaghetti, pasta pieces such as twists (huge choice – get the ones you like), lasagna sheets. Tinned spaghetti hoops, tinned Bolognese, macaroni cheese. Instant noodles.
Staples	Dried rice, couscous, quinoa. Convenience microwave / easy heat rice in whichever flavours you like or get a selection. Mashed potato powder.
Cereals	Oats, cereal variety packs (buy on offer- one per family member so they can trade their favourites), large boxes of whatever cereal your family likes.
Meat and Fish	Tinned tuna, salmon, sausages, hot dogs, meatballs, sardines, mackerel, chicken, corned beef, ham, mince, hot dogs. Sandwich paste. Longlife on the shelf pates.

Vegetables	Tinned tomatoes, tomato puree, garlic puree, carrots, peas, potatoes, artichokes, olives, sundried tomatoes, courgettes, mushrooms, aubergine, jalopenos. Dried mushrooms. Jarred lemon slices.
Fruit	Dried fruit- apricots, sultanas, raisins. Tinned fruit- fruit cocktail, pears, pineapple, peaches, mandarin, grapefruit, berries. Frozen berries, rhubarb, apple slices for cooking with.
Breads	Crackers, crisp breads, bread flour, yeast.
Preserves and spreads	Jams, marmalades, pickles, branded items you like e.g. Nutella and Biscoff. Chutneys.
Condiments	Tomato ketchup, mayonnaise, mustards, chilli sauces, anything else you like with food. These tend to have a long shelf life.
Store cupboard ingredients	Salt, pepper, herbs, spices, chilli sauces, soy sauce, stock cubes, gravy granules, lemon juice, tinned or block coconut- these will all help you make what you cook flavorsome and appealing so make sure you have plenty.

Store cupboard ingredients (cont.)	Corn flour to thicken soups is useful too. They don't take up too much room. Tahini is also useful if you like hummus.
Cooking fats and oils	Olive oil, sunflower oil and vegetable oil. Olive oil is likely to become hard to get and expensive- supermarket own versions are far cheaper than branded. If olive oil gets cold when stored it can look like it is going solid but is fine when in a warmer room again. Ghee (comes in tins so great shelf life and useful to cook with).
Cooking sauces	Tomato pasta sauce, pesto sauce, white sauce (for making lasagne but also good for other pasta dishes), curry sauces (different flavours for variety and if different family members have different curry preferences), Chinese sauces e.g. sweet and sour. These all come in jars so are good to store and last well. Look at what is on offer or at supermarket own versions to reduce cost. Packet sauces e.g. cheese sauce, white sauce.
Soups	Packet soups which just need water, tinned soups. Soups are very useful- they are easy to prepare and eat, a source of fluid and will help towards dietary vegetable intake.

Soups (cont.)	Some soups can be bulked out with other ingredients to make a more substantial meal. Tins will last a long time. If you want to make your own soups, consider purchasing a stick blender- they can be bought cheaply and are very useful to have.
Dairy	Long life milk, powdered milk. Soya milk (has a much longer shelf life than regular long life milk so a useful addition to your stockpile), tinned evaporated milk, condensed milk, longlife cheese spreads, look at soya cheeses too. Long lasting cheese such as Stilton, Parmesan. Block butter to put in the fridge, if bought closer to Brexit time should last a while, you can also freeze it. You can put cream into an ice cube tray so you can use a cube or two for cooking if needed. Just defrost in a ramekin or similar.
Flour and Baking	Flour of all types you would use, yeast packets, sugar, any other baking ingredients. Consider investing in a bread machine too (can be bought cheaply second hand).

Flour and Baking (cont.)	Flour doesn't have a very long shelf life, put the packets in sealed plastic bags and freeze for a few days to extend their lifespan (kills any weevil larvae that may be present) then remove and store. Premade pizza dough / dumpling mixes. Look at powdered egg although this can be hard to get hold of but could be useful if eggs are unavailable.
Sugar and Sweet things	Sugar (all types you would use), golden syrup (cheap and very useful), honey, maple syrup, sweeteners if you use them. Cocoa powder. Cooking chocolate.
Hot drinks	Coffee- instant or ground or both (supermarket own can save money here). Teabags, hot chocolate.
Cold drinks	Canned drinks that you like (be very careful checking dates with these, some have a long life others are surprisingly short), longlife fruit juices that can be kept on the shelf.
Desserts and Puddings	Tinned rice pudding, syrup puddings, tinned custard, sticky toffee puddings, jelly cubes or ready made jelly pots.

Desserts and Puddings (cont.)	Some potted desserts that are kept on the shelf have long best before dates although can be expensive. Lots of evaporated milk, tinned fruit, condensed milk.
Treats	Chocolate bars, biscuits, long life cakes- in terms of morale these will help your family if you get the ones they like as an occasional treat. Check dates- large variation between different products.

Tinned Meals

As well as all the foods suggested above, there is an increasing range of tinned meals that just need heating before serving. They can either be eaten on their own or with some rice or pasta.

Some of the different meals available include Curries (huge variety available), Chilli con carne, Bolognese sauce, Irish Stew, Minced Beef and Gravy, Chicken in White Sauce, Spaghetti Bolognese (the pasta and the sauce), meatballs, sweet and sour chicken, meat pies, haggis and various others depending on where you look.

There is also a good range of jarred meals available in many supermarkets which are worth looking at.

Having a few tinned or jarred meals that can be turned into dinner in a very short space of time along with a quick side is very useful. If we are going to be surviving on our stockpile, it is likely that there are going to be days when we are exhausted from what we are living through and not having to cook a whole meal from scratch will be a welcome break. Alternatively, they can be used as a base to create other meals with the addition of further items from your supplies if you are up to some cooking.

If buying tins or jars like this, decide how many you think you need for a meal for your household- if you need three (for a family of two adults and one or two children for example) buy three or multiples of three so that you don't end up with odd leftover tins or go back to get more and find they've run out.

Foods for the Fridge and Freezer

As explained elsewhere in the book, fridges and freezers shouldn't be relied upon as a source of storage as they are vulnerable to power cuts. However, there is no harm in using them as long as you make sure your supplies could work if you lost what was in the fridge or freezer if the power went off for too long. The fridge or freezer give the option of adding variety and a few extra meals and ingredients to your stockpile.

Suggested items for fridges and freezers are below. Again, these are not an exhaustive list and you should use it to give you ideas about what you would want to store in yours. If you can allocate a specific shelf to your prepping stores that will keep it all together so it is easier to see what you have and also to keep it from being eaten before it should be.

Fridge
- Butter, spreadable butter, lard.
- Block cheeses and longer life cheeses: Cheddar, Parmesan and anything else you like.
- Long life cheese- some cheese spreads have up to 10 months date on them so if you like cheese spreads it's worth putting some of these in the fridge.
- Pepperami and similar. They have a very long date on them and versatile for cooking with as well as just eating. Look out for them on offer.
- Preserved meats e.g. salami, chorizo.
- More bottled water if there is spare space
- Long life milk
- Anything else you like that you can keep in the fridge with a reasonably long shelf life.

Freezer
- Block butter, lard. Both freeze well. Chop a block of butter and put the chunks in a bag so you have a knob of butter ready to take out if you need one for cooking rather than having to take the whole block out.
- Cheese: some varieties work better than others and will come out crumbly but fine to cook with. Parmesan, blocks of Cheddar, Stilton, Boursin all freeze well and can be used to liven up many different dishes.
- Meat: Variety of meat cuts that will cook well following being frozen and that can be made into lots of different meals for variety. An example selection would be: Beef mince, chicken breasts, chicken thighs, gammon joint, sandwich steaks, beef joint (e.g. brisket), stewing steak, chorizo chunks, bacon lardons, pancetta, sausages.

Consider removing meats from their packaging and resealing in plastic bags to make better use of the space available. Resealable packs of pate are inexpensive and useful to have in the freezer.

- Vegetables: Chopped mushrooms and chopped onions. Both freeze and then cook well and are very versatile so can be used in cooking many dishes. Packs of frozen vegetables that you like from the supermarket that will work with your other items to cook meals with. Carrots, peas, spinach, sweetcorn are all useful to have as are broccoli and cauliflower. Chopped celery is useful to have in the freezer for cooking with as are sliced peppers and garlic cloves.

- Fruit: Fresh rhubarb freezes well as do apples- if you grow them it's definitely worth freezing them as they can be used to make a crumble straight from the freezer. Frozen berries are not too expensive at the moment, give lots of cooking options and are likely to be an item that increases in price. Put slices of lemon flat on a baking sheet to freeze and then seal in a plastic bag so that you have lemon slices available for drinks or cooking with if fresh lemons become unavailable.

- Frozen ready-made pastry.

- Milk: freezes well but make sure to squeeze some of the air from the bottle and reseal to give room for it to expand as it freezes. An additional benefit is that it will help keep freezer cold for longer if the power goes off.

- Water: as mentioned elsewhere, it could be useful to have some water stored in the freezer to help keep it cold if the power goes off as well as providing an extra few litres of water that are stored. As for milk, squeeze the air from the bottle and reseal prior to freezing to allow room for expansion as it freezes.
- Batch cooked meals: If you have suitable containers to store them in and are cooking suitable meals such as Bolognese, chilli con carne, stews or casseroles consider making double portions and freezing one. Premade meals like this could be a welcome addition to your stores but remember they will need defrosting thoroughly and properly heating before you can eat them.
- Bread: A couple of frozen loaves will be useful in taking up freezer space to keep it cooler longer if the power goes off, and bread is also good to use once frozen particularly if toasting it. Packs of part-baked bread would be a nice addition as are any spare freezable cakes if you happen to bake them or pick them up on offer at the supermarket.

7- What to Buy: Non Food Items

As well as food and water, we all need a variety of non-food supplies and consumables to go about our daily lives. Whilst we won't starve to death if we run out of toilet roll, life will be much more pleasant if we have plenty available.

This chapter gives ideas on non-food items that you may wish to stock up on. As with the other items in the book, trading down to other brands or shops can save a significant amount of money to help make the process more affordable.

<u>Everyday Items</u>

Tin Opener
Obvious but easily overlooked- prepping is almost inevitably going to involve a lot of tins. Even if you have a tin opener (a surprising number of people these days don't), it would do no harm to get another as a spare. Keep it with your stockpile so you always know where it is. Even better, get two. They can be bought quite cheaply and if you remember that you need it to access a large amount of your stockpile you will see why it is so expensive to ensure you have one available when you need it.

Cash
If Brexit hits badly, nobody really knows what the consequences will be. There have been a few incidents in the last few years where the IT systems of banks went down and their customers were unable to use their cards to pay or access their funds for a few days.

Who knows if this could happen post Brexit, how long it would last and the scale of the problems. If you can get a bit of cash put by then you would have at least some reserves to use if required until the systems were working again. Hopefully if your prepping goes to plan, you wouldn't need to go to the shops for much food but for other essentials such as bus fares, petrol, school dinners and all the other everyday expenses that crop up it could save a lot of trouble if you could had cash available to cover this type of thing without worrying about when you could use your bank card again.

Lighting, Heating and Power

This is covered in more detail in the chapter on Useful Equipment, but in brief:
-   Torch(es) and plenty of batteries
-   LED battery and wind up light(s)
-   Some way of heating food and liquid if the power goes down
-   Power bank or other way to keep your mobile phone charged if the power goes down

Bathroom
-   Toilet Rolls
-   Soap
-   Handwash
-   Shower Gel / Bubble Bath
-   Shampoo
-   Conditioner (if you use it)
-   Other hair products if required
-   Spare toothbrush(es)
-   Toothpaste
-   Deodorant / antiperspirant

- Moisturiser
- Make up (if you use it)
- Sanitary products as required
- Any specific items that may be required by family members (very young or very old)
- Wipes (baby wipes or you can get bed bath wipes for invalids online) – in case the power / water goes down and showers aren't possible for any length of time.

Kitchen
- Kitchen roll
- Cleaning cloths
- Washing up liquid (even if you have a dishwasher just in case power goes off)
- Cleaning products
- Laundry products (including those you could use to wash by hand if necessary)
- Dishwasher tablets

It's important not to keep chemicals or detergents next to your food supplies. Perhaps you could clear an area in the cupboard under your sink or somewhere else away from your food stockpile. A plastic storage box would be useful in keeping everything together- you could have one for bathroom products and one for kitchen products.

Medicine Cupboard

This First Aid and personal medications advice is a common-sense approach. Ensure you are happy with your preparations, and level of knowledge, and consult a medical professional if in doubt. The Author offers this advice as common sense and it should be taken as such.

We should all have at least a small medicine cupboard with a few essentials such as paracetamol. If you don't have one, this is a good opportunity to review what you have and add to it as well as creating one in your supplies. **Please be very aware that medicines should be kept out of the reach of children and take this into account when storing it.**

This list gives many possibilities for a home medicine cupboard-use it to create your own list. It would be better to have too many items and feel prepared for more situations than to have a situation that you weren't prepared for. If Brexit is as bad as some fear, the country will be under a huge amount of pressure as a whole and this may extend to emergency and health services. Being able to avoid a trip to the doctor or hospital for an ailment that could be treated at home would be an advantage.

Useful items to start off your medicine cupboard that can be obtained over the counter at the chemist should be:
- Antihistamines: Chloraphenamine (Piriton), especially if you have children. Also Cetirizine which has the main advantage that it is non drowsy but covers a smaller range of things.
- Simple analgesics: Paracetamol, Solpadeine, Ibuprofen.
- Steroid cream: For rashes and bites etc.

- Antiseptics.

Other items which may be useful:
- Antiseptic e.g. TCP
- Aspirin
- Buscopan
- Calpol
- Canistan cream
- Cold / flu tablets (careful with amount of paracetamol)
- Contraceptives if required
- Dioralyte or other rehydration treatment
- Echinacea
- Gaviscon or other heartburn / indigestion remedy
- Immodium
- Karvol (for children but can be handy for adults too)
- Laxatives
- Milk of magnesia
- Nasal spray
- Nit treatment if you have children
- Nurofen
- Optrex / chloramphenicol
- Sudocrem
- Throat spray
- Vicks Vapour Rub
- Voltarol
- Witch Hazel

Vitamins

If you're prepping with the assumption that any food shortages and difficulties are only for a week or so, then vitamins aren't necessary as a week living on your supplies won't cause any damage. If, however you want to build supplies to last a month or more then you should add vitamins to the stockpile.

However well you prep in terms of having fruit and vegetables, if we have serious shortages of fresh fruit and vegetables (it has been suggested that these are one of the most threatened food groups since so much is imported from abroad, and much of what we pick no longer has the labour here to pick it), a diet without these is likely to risk vitamin deficiencies. Vitamins can be picked up cheaply if you go with supermarket own value ranges and have a long shelf life so can be added to your supplies early on. It won't cost much to buy enough to last your family 2-3 months just in case and is well worth it in terms of peace of mind for everyone's health. Even if you're only prepping for a week, it wouldn't do any harm to have some vitamins stashed away just in case fresh fruit and vegetables become hard to obtain for longer than expected.

First Aid

Everyone should have a First Aid kit in the house, even if only a basic one. Small basic ones can be bought from Amazon or eBay very cheaply. If nothing else, buy one of these and then add more items to it. They are so cheap you could buy two- one for your normal medicine cupboard and the other for your stockpile to ensure it isn't used up and not replaced.

Basic First Aid items:
- Alcohol-free cleansing wipes
- Antihistamine tablets

- Antiseptic cream
- Cough medicine
- Cream or spray to relieve insect bites and stings
- Crêpe rolled bandages
- Disposable sterile gloves
- Distilled water for cleaning wounds
- Eye wash and eye bath
- Painkillers such as paracetamol (or infant paracetamol for children), aspirin (not to be given to children under 16), or ibuprofen
- Plasters in various different sizes and shapes
- Safety pins
- Sanitary towels- for dealing with bleeding injuries
- Scissors
- Skin rash cream, such as hydrocortisone or calendula
- Sterile gauze dressings in different sizes
- Sterile eye dressings (at least 2)
- Sticky tape
- Thermometer (preferably digital)
- Triangular bandages
- Tweezers

You could also add face shields or pocket masks (for giving mouth to mouth) and clingfilm in case of having to treat burns.

The most important thing you should add to your First Aid Kit is a First Aid book. Read it when you purchase it and then keep it with the First Aid Kit. If you need to refer to it to deliver First Aid at least you will have read it already and it will be familiar even if you don't remember the detail- rather than having an accident to deal with and then having to try and find the right part of the book to help you in an emergency situation. Reading it when you get it will also give you ideas of any more advanced First Aid equipment that you might want to add to your stocks. Remember, apps and internet searches are great unless the internet goes off for any reason- it is a good idea to have a book that is there if needed.

Prescription Drugs
Many people are understandably concerned about what will happen with the drugs they get on prescription, particularly in light of the public announcements that the NHS is stockpiling some drugs in case of supply shortages post Brexit.

It seems that arrangements are being made to stockpile prescription drugs that are licensed for use in the UK (they would have to be to be prescribed here) that come into the country from Europe (although not the Republic of Ireland).

Some drugs can't be stockpiled due to their short shelf lives – the Government has asked suppliers arrange for these to be air freighted into the country post Brexit if required. Whether planes will be flying by then of course depends on the air regulations and agreements being sorted in time...

Wanting to start your own stockpile of your medication is understandable given the unpredictability of the current situation but unfortunately is very difficult. It's illegal to give prescription medication to other people (so you couldn't legally give a course of medication the doctor had taken you off and you still had some left to a friend who was on it without it being illegal).

Some people are trying to build up a small buffer of medication by reordering repeat prescriptions a day or two earlier each time and gaining a few extra days' worth of medication over time by using the First In First Out method.
If this reassures you and you're going to use it anyway it seems fairly harmless but be warned that surgeries and pharmacies are becoming more aware of this practice as well as that of asking for a replacement for "lost" medication to give a larger stockpile.

Some people may be aware of online companies that claim to sell prescription drugs. If these appeal to you, feel free to investigate but be warned that they have a dubious reputation, are unregulated and there is no way to be sure that what you get is what you actually ordered. The author would not recommend purchasing from these companies and it would most definitely be a case of buyer beware. The peace of mind in having extra drugs from these companies would be cancelled out for most people by the uncertainty that they may not be the right drugs at all.

8- Where to Buy Your Supplies

Where you get your supplies depends in part on how you wish to do your stockpiling. If you want to add a few items to your weekly shop then you will be purchasing from wherever you are doing your normal shopping. If you would prefer to do a few big shopping trips specifically for building your stockpile then it is worth considering carefully which shops you go to. If you have time, and are within reasonable distance of a variety of shops it could be worthwhile to investigate the prices of items you intend to bulk buy at different shops so that you know the best available price locally.

Whether you shop gradually or all at once depends on your ability to fund a big shopping trip all at once and also how quickly you want to build up your stockpile. You might decide to do a combination so do a large shop initially and then add a few more items to it whenever you do your normal shop.

Consider "trading down" to make your money go further in your shopping. Whether that is by trading down from branded food to supermarket own, or from your current supermarket to a budget retailer is up to you but it can save a lot of money which means you can build your stockpile more quickly so is definitely worth doing.

Take advantage of any products being on offer such as Buy One Get One Free but double check that the price is competitive- supermarkets can be naughty and make these offers seem better than they really are but increasing the price of the one you buy. Always check the price per gram (usually on the price label on the shelf or on the internet listing if online) to let you compare different products and to make sure you are getting the best deal.

If you trade down now for day to day shopping as well as your big stockpile shopping trip this will be helpful as it will:

- Allow you to check that you like what you are purchasing (no point buying 20 tins of Spam if your family refuse to eat it and you won't eat any of it day to day).
- Make your money go further so will offset the cost of your prepping to some degree and allow you to build your stockpile more quickly.

Wherever you purchase your supplies from, ensure that you check the Best Before date on each to make sure they have a sufficiently long date. While most tinned and long life products have long dates it is possible to be caught out and find some with less than a year on them. Unless you are sure you are going to rotate these through your normal food consumption it may be better to get an alternative with a longer date rather than risk them going out of date if you don't want to eat tins beyond their Best Before date.

Some ideas for where to purchase your supplies are detailed below:

Supermarkets

Many supermarkets have good value or own brand ranges which are very useful for stockpiling with. Tesco, Asda and Morrisons all offer a wide variety of products at reasonable prices.

If you are going to use supermarkets to stockpile with it is worth bearing in mind a couple of factors:

- Smaller "convenience" shops will be more expensive than the larger supermarkets even if they are the same company. On some items this can be a couple of pence, on others significantly more. It might be a price worth paying if you are popping in to pick something up for dinner on the way back from work but is an unnecessary expense for a larger scale shopping trip. As an example of the price differences between these shops, my local "convenience" shop has 2 litre bottles of water at 49p each. In their larger store less than a mile away, the same bottles of water are 19p- a huge difference so it is worth knowing how much things are in the different shops and going to the one that works best in terms of price for your shopping.

- Online grocery ordering and home delivery is a helpful option for many people. If you live a few miles away this can work really well as it saves you the cost and time of the journey for the sake of a small delivery charge and you could potentially build up a large stockpile in just a couple of orders. It is worth bearing in mind though that when you do the order online, the shops often do not display the entire selection they stock for that product. Usually it is the cheaper products that don't always appear as options on the online ordering system. If you are saving a large amount of time and money in terms of a journey to get to the shop (online grocery shopping can be a lifeline if you live in a rural area) then you may not mind this. But if you are within a reasonable distance of a large superstore it is worth visiting to benefit from the full selection of products. If you are a regular online shopper and know what is and isn't available on the online ordering system you could compromise by ordering what you can with your online shopping but doing a physical trip to the shop to stock up on other items that aren't available to purchase online. If you join a new supermarket's online shopping scheme, you can sometimes get sizeable discounts on your first order so this is worth looking into to see if it would save you money.

Discount stores

Aldi and Lidl are the prepper's best friend! Both offer a great range of products at very reasonable prices. If you have both locally it is worth checking them both out as they do have different ranges but you can save a large amount of money stockpiling in these shops and picking up the few bits they don't do elsewhere rather than shopping in a normal supermarket, especially a higher end one.

Aldi are brilliant for olive oil, pasta, pulses, tinned vegetables and pet food. Lidl are great for tinned vegetables (with some more interesting varieties) and meat. Both have a wide range so if you only have one nearby it is definitely worth paying a visit. If you have both, if time allows, check out both and you may end up buying some products from one and others from the other.

As well as Aldi and Lidl, which are discount supermarkets, there are other discount stores such as B&M and Home Bargains. These are worth looking at as although they have a smaller range of food stuffs, they sometimes have interesting end of line long life foods that the other shops may not stock at very cheap prices. It would be difficult to build an entire stockpile from these shops but they can be a good source of extra bits and bobs to add variety to what you have. As for all shopping for stockpiling, ensure you check the dates on each item are long enough for your needs.

Road Trip

People used to drive to the nearest part of France / Europe they could get to from the UK on Booze Cruises. These may be out of fashion now, but for anyone for whom this sort of road trip is possible, a supplies shopping trip could be an option. French hypermarkets have all sorts of lovely long- life foods that we don't have in this country (although you can order some by using specialist websites). If it is feasible in terms of distance, cost and having a large enough vehicle to make it worthwhile it's a tempting option. If doing this, prioritise items that we either can't just pick up at the shops in this country, or those that are significantly cheaper than here.

Online Shopping

As well as online supermarket shopping where you order online and they pick your order from the supermarket and deliver it to you, there are a number of companies that do mail order for various food products. Some offer discounted food that is approaching or past the best before date, others stock highly specialist products that would be expensive to rely on alone but can provide variety to your stockpile and are useful if you wish to source a specific food to store.

The best known discount retailer is Approved Foods (**www.ApprovedFoods.co.uk**). They sell a huge variety of products with the range changing all the time. It is important to understand that the majority of their products are near or past their best before dates. There is an important distinction between Use By dates- beyond which a product should not be eaten; and Best Before dates- which give an indication of time but beyond which the product is almost certainly still going to be perfectly usable.

Stored correctly, tins and jars can last years beyond their Best Before dates. If you are happy to have food that has exceeded the Best Before date, you may find some real bargains on this website which could boost your stockpile comparatively cheaply. Before getting carried away on the site (very easy to do), remind yourself only to buy food you are sure will be used so that you don't end up with a cupboard full of food that was ridiculously cheap but that you will never actually eat which would be a waste both of your money and the storage space. That said, if you can restrain yourself to what you actually use day to day, it is definitely worth having a look at. Discounts vary between items- some are small but some can be huge.

Specialist websites selling food from particular countries also exist. Website suggestions are listed below- these are a good place to start to see what is available online but readers should satisfy themselves that they are happy with any website they intend to purchase from prior to doing so, and should note that there are other similar retailers also available on the internet.

https://www.frenchclick.co.uk/ - French food

https://italianfooddistribution.co.uk/ Italian

https://germandeli.co.uk/ German

https://delicioso.co.uk/shop-online/ Spanish

http://www.thegreekdeli.com Greek

http://www.krakowsky.co.uk/ Polish

https://babushkadeli.uk Russian (huge selection of prepping friendly food)

https://www.waiyeehong.com/ Chinese

https://www.veenas.com Indian

As well as the above retailers for food products, Amazon and eBay have such large ranges that they can be a good source for some foods as well as pretty much any non-food and prepping equipment you can think of.

9- Where to Put Your Stockpile

Depending on how many supplies you wish to have stored, you may need additional storage. There are a surprising number of places around the house that are possible options.

One of the key themes in setting up your storage has to be ensuring it is secure. Hunger makes people do bad things and although we hope it won't happen if the worst case scenario occurred there is the potential for largescale civil unrest. This means you would want your food and supplies to be tucked away where unwanted visitors would be unlikely to find them.

Have storage in mind as you purchase items for your stockpile. Any stockpiling is almost certainly going to have a large number of tins. Tins are good to store as they are small enough to fit in many different places. They are also relatively robust in their storage requirements. Don't buy the large catering size tins unless your family is large enough to eat the contents in one go- remember if the power went down you wouldn't be able to refrigerate any leftovers which could go to waste. The standard individual sized tins are better in terms of no wastage, ease of use and storage. When buying tins, ensure you check the condition of each- as well as checking the date, make sure that they aren't dented or damaged as this can significantly reduce their shelf life.

This chapter gives ideas on places around the house- some obvious and some less so, that could be utilised for storing your supplies as well as some ideas to add to your stockpile without taking up too much extra space.

Storing Food

In terms of storing larger quantities of pulses, rice, pasta etc. you can either keep them bagged as they are (but they would have to be somewhere 100% clear of rodents) or consider using glass jars. Glass jars in a dark place can help them last longer.

Serious preppers will use mylar bags and / or oxygen removing tablets with glass jars- either of these can make rice and grains last significantly longer. Mylar bags and oxygen removing tablets might be a bridge too far for many people reading this book, if this does appeal it's easy to source both the method and the required materials on the internet. Glass jars however are useful even to the new Brexit prepper- they do make it easier to see how much you have of each thing. If you want to do this just make sure the jars are clean and totally dry before filling them, and make sure they are stored where they can't fall down. Pressing down slightly on the contents with clean utensil or hand will compress them so you can fit more in.

If you wish to preserve food as well as just purchase long life items, look into dehydrating and canning. Dehydrating requires the use of a dehydrator which can be bought easily online. Prices vary but make sure you check the reviews when choosing which one to purchase.

Canning can be done in various ways depending on what is being canned. Fruit and vegetables are easier to do than meat which requires the use of a pressure cooker. Again, sets of equipment can be purchased online if this is something you wish to pursue. There are a variety of books and websites detailing how to do dehydration and canning if these are something you would like to know more about.

Dried vegetables can be purchased online or in specialist food shops. These are a useful addition to a stockpile as they can add versatility to cooking- in soups, stews etc. and have the huge advantage that because they are dried, they take up very little space compared to when they rehydrate. Being dried also gives them a long shelf life. The only disadvantage of course is that they need water to dehydrate in, but assuming water isn't an issue this won't cause a problem so they are well worth looking at as an extra addition that is very efficient space wise and versatile in what it can be used for.

<u>Where to put it: Kitchen</u>

In Plain Sight
This means keeping it along with your usual food. This would mean buying extra items of everything such as tinned food / olive oil etc. so that instead of having one in the cupboard you have two. This is useful as it can increase the amount of food you have in your cupboards on a day to day basis so creates a good buffer in case you can't get to the shops for any reason for a day or two. This method relies on you changing your shopping methods so that the moment you have run out of the one you are using, you replace it so there is always a "spare" one in the cupboard.

The risk with this of course is using it up and not replacing and ending up with very little extra food "in stock". Or a family member using it up without asking. Having your cupboards with larger quantities of your day to day food is a good idea if possible but this method would probably not work as your only storage option.

If you decide to do this, ensure that you rotate your stock so the oldest ones are always used first to ensure you have the longest lasting food in your cupboards.

One benefit of using this method is that if anyone noticed you were buying more food you could stay you were stocking up and it would be obvious from your cupboards that you had ample supplies in. This would hopefully discourage people from wondering where you were storing your additional food and going looking for it if food shortages were to happen. In the worst case scenario if people came trying to steal supplies they would find the food in the cupboard which would hopefully stop them looking elsewhere for the rest of (and majority of) your supplies.

Kitchen Cupboards
If you have a few kitchen cupboards, you may be able to have a sort out and rearrange things so that you can give one (or half of one) over to prepping. This is a nice way to start prepping and would probably suffice for the 3-day emergency stash.

Some cupboards don't go all the way up to the ceiling so for these there is the potential to use the cupboard tops. This needs to be done reasonably carefully- you wouldn't want to put really heavy items on there in case the load was too much and caused the cupboards to come down. You also would not want it to be obvious what you were doing so one good way of utilizing this space is to get some nice storage boxes to put on top of the cupboards. Packets such as pasta, rice, instant dried soup would go well in the boxes so they weren't too heavy for the cupboards or to be got down when needed.

If your kitchen cupboards are the sort with the "lip" around them at the top, you may find that the space created behind is deep enough for things like packets of spaghetti laid flat so you could use the space without buying storage boxes, Tops of cupboards are great as they are inaccessible to mice or rats so a are very useful place to put packets as long as it isn't too difficult to retrieve items when needed.

"Round the corner" cupboards- many modern kitchens have one of these to maximize storage in the kitchen. These are useful as although it can be a fiddle to get to, there is an area "round the corner" and therefore not immediately obvious to anyone looking in it. You could certainly get a few tins in the furthest away part which could then free up storage space elsewhere for other things.

The cupboard under the sink- these are often large so could potentially take a reasonable amount of supplies. The key thing to remember is that you shouldn't keep your food supplies next to detergents and other chemicals. This means that your under sink cupboard is out of bounds for food, but if you cleared it out you could probably make room for many nonfood supplies that you wanted to store such as candles, batteries, torches or additional cleaning products.

Kickboards
Most kitchens have a panel underneath the lower cupboards to cover the gap between the cupboard and the floor. Don't go ripping them off willy-nilly, but many are set up so that they can be easily removed and replaced. If yours are like this, you will find there is a handy area behind them which is sufficient to store bottles of water or plenty of tins. It is surprising how

much will fit in there. Before using this area, ensure that it is properly clean and with no signs of vermin. Regularly review it and only put tins in there rather than running the risk of attracting vermin. If you intend to put bottled water in there, place some carpet or similar down rather than storing them on the concrete. If you want to put other food stuffs / packets in the space, put them into metal containers (biscuit tins are perfect) to make sure vermin can't smell them or get into them. Using this area as storage is a well-known prepper "trick". Some readers will find it useful, others will not- decide what is best for you.

Fridge and Freezer
Fridges and freezers are fantastic for storing supplies but you must remember that they are vulnerable to power cuts- if the power goes off for too long then there is a risk that the food will spoil. For this reason, they should be utilised but not relied upon as a sole or even main method of storage. By all means have plenty of supplies in the freezer but be sure that you have sufficient stocks stored in different ways to allow you to survive if the freezer went down and you lost its contents.

Fridge
If you have one fridge then you will be using it all the time and this makes it difficult to store too much in it for the longer term. However if you can set aside a back corner of a shelf, you may be able to store a few items such as long life cheese or cheese spreads which you can rotate through your stocks so that you always have the longest shelf life food stored in the fridge.

Some households have a second fridge, often stored in the garage or utility room- often used for drinks and other items which are not required on a daily basis (or they'd be in the kitchen fridge). Having an extra fridge which is not accessed all the time by all of the family gives more scope for storage possibilities but ensure that stock rotation is done regularly and that the contents you have stored in there are not forgotten about.

Freezer
Depending on the amount of freezer storage available, freezers can be a hugely useful storage resource.

Guarding against Power Failures
If you are going to use the freezer to store supplies, it is important to know how to protect your supplies to reduce the risk of them being spoiled in the event of interruptions to the power supply.

- Try to keep your freezer reasonably full although still with room for air to circulate. A full freezer will remain colder for longer than a half empty freezer. Loaves of bread are good for using up freezer space to keep it full at a reasonable cost and are obviously useful to have if needed.
- Keep some bottles of water in the freezer. They will help to maintain the cold temperature in the event of a power cut and having them provides an extra few litres of water should your water supplies be interrupted. Before freezing water, open the bottle and squeeze it a little before replacing the lid tightly. This will allow room for the water to expand as it freezes without breaking the bottle. You can also do this with milk.
- If you want to see how much the contents of a freezer have defrosted in a power cut, you could freeze a small container of water in the middle of it. Once frozen, put a penny or

button on top of the frozen water and replace in the freezer. If there is a power cut and you are worried about how much the freezer contents may have defrosted, you can see if the penny remains where you put it (so the water didn't melt) or if it has sunk down (indicating that the water has melted and refrozen).

- If there is a power cut:
  - Don't Panic!
  - Don't open the freezer!

If the power goes off, it is vitally important not to open the freezer (or fridge). The moment the door is opened, even once, it will increase the temperature within the freezer. If you have any blankets or a spare duvet, consider putting these around or over the freezer. You want to insulate it to keep cold contained within the freezer to stop it warming up and thawing out. If you do this, and don't open the freezer at all there is a good chance that it will stay frozen for 24-48 hours without power if it is full (a half empty freezer would thaw more rapidly).

Many power cuts only go on for a few hours. Using the methods detailed above, your freezer and its contents should survive that amount of time without power with no problems. If power does become an issue post Brexit (there are suggestions that it may do due to energy supply agreements with Europe), if these manifest as power cuts lasting a few hours but no more this is survivable. If power cuts go on for days then this is more of a worry. Remember though that food in the freezer is still going to be cold but after a longer period of time will defrost. If you decide to open the freezer to assess the contents, if the contents are defrosted but still cold then they are still usable.

You may find that contents near the door are defrosted but those towards the back or the bottom are not. Don't panic and throw everything out, anything that is defrosted but still "fridge cold" should be usable so rather than throw it out you should use it but obviously assess the quality of each item to ensure you are happy to use it. You could use a food thermometer to check whether the food is still "fridge cold" to help you assess each item. If the defrosted items are raw meat and you are satisfied that they are safe to use, you can cook them into a meals such as curry or casserole and freeze the meal.

Supplies you could consider storing in the freezer include:
- Milk and Water (as explained above)
- Bread- It's useful to have one or two frozen loaves if space allows. They will also help keep the freezer cold if the power goes off. Frozen bread can be toasted or defrosted easily so is useful to have to hand. You could also put part baked bread packs in there.
- Cheese -some types freeze better than others but it can be frozen and be suitable to cook with once thawed
- Pate- Homemade pate can be frozen. With the frozen bread this gives the makings of pate on toast very easily as a simple and different meal.
- Meats- If you eat meat, it is sensible to have some meat frozen to give a bit of variety in your diet if your supplies are needed. Meat is also likely to increase in price so is a worthwhile investment in terms of providing a buffer against future price rises in your day to day living. Having a selection of different cuts and types of meat would allow you to create a selection of different meals. Your selection could have mince, chicken breasts /

fillets, frying steaks, sausages, burgers, gammon joint, cheap beef joint or anything else you would eat (so you can rotate through your usual food consumption) and that is relatively easy to cook with.

- Fish- If you eat fish, again it could be sensible to have some stored to add variety to your diet should you need to use your supplies but it is important to ensure you rotate frozen food through your normal food consumption for maximum shelf life and minimal wastage.
- Vegetables
- Batch cooked meals
- Block butter
- Treats- if you can stretch to it, a couple of treats that freeze well is worth putting in. If it comes to using the Brexit supplies, it will be important to maintain morale so if your family has a favourite ice cream or other frozen treat it would come as a welcome treat.

Cellar / Basement

If you are lucky enough to have a cellar or basement, this is an obvious place to consider storing your supplies. Before you begin, ensure that the area you intend to use is clean and dry and rodent free (with no obvious way in for them either). Setting up a set of shelves or two is easily done and perfectly usable shelves can be obtained very cheaply via second hand selling sites or shops or brand new from retailers such as Argos or Amazon. Go for sturdy shelves that will take plenty of weight or repurpose any spare ones you might have around the house. Make sure the shelves are securely on the floor (cellar floors can be uneven) so that they do not risk toppling over with the weight of your supplies. You could create mountings from the wall to the top of the shelves for safety if this was a concern. Another good source of shelving units is IKEA. Their tall, thin shelves (designed for DVDs / CDs) have a tiny footprint but take an impressive amount of tins and other bits and bobs. Their range of shelves that come in squares (configurations of 2,4,8 etc.) with fabric "drawers" to go into the squares hold a fantastic amount so are brilliant for storage. As an added bonus, if you use them with the fabric inners, this will conceal the fact you are storing food in them. As they are so popular, both of these types of shelves are often for sale second hand or aren't too expensive new if you are within a reasonable distance of IKEA.

The cellar is a good place to store supplies as it is out of the way of visitors so people won't see that you are building a stockpile. Ensure that there is a good source of light down there, and perhaps leave a charged torch down there in case the power happened to go off when you were in the cellar. Keep an eye on the temperature in the cellar- it should stay cool in summer but if it gets too cold in winter you may wish to move some supplies to other areas if you are worried they would suffer.

Cupboard Under the Stairs
The cupboard under the stairs if you have one is a great place for storage- they are usually a decent sized space and in the centre of the house so well protected against the elements. The majority would have room for a set of shelves, if they haven't already got them. Even a small shelf unit or some plastic boxes at the furthest away point of the cupboard behind day to day items would provide some useful storage and not be obvious to visitors.

Living Room

Your living room (or other downstairs room such as dining room / family room etc) is likely to have potential for some storage. Some people conceal tins under or behind their sofas. Others use coffee and side tables or sideboards that have a large amount of internal storage. Each individual item may not store that many tins or items of food but they will add up. Remember though, that the more well hidden the items are, the easier it is to forget they are there and not rotate them through your normal eating so in the long term there would be a risk they might go out of date. This is where good record keeping comes in, so that you can see what you have and don't forget to use it in time.

Bedrooms

Bedrooms have lots of potential for storage. If they are upstairs, remember to be careful carrying heavy items upstairs.

- Wardrobes:
    - Items can be stored on top of wardrobes if you can reach safely. Some have a "lip" around the top creating a small space that you could put items in where they wouldn't be seen. Or you could (similarly as for kitchen cupboards) buy storage boxes that co-ordinate with the bedroom and will hold a reasonable amount of supplies without showing the contents.
    - Rearranging the bottom of the wardrobe would create room for a couple of rows of tins at least, or more stylish storage boxes to hold supplies. This would still give room to store day to day items.

- Under the bed:
    - Divan style beds have a huge amount of storage space within them. It would be sensible to use the clear plastic boxes so you can easily see what you have in there. A large amount of food could easily be concealed in this way.
    - Non divan beds often have room for something under the bed. Storage boxes would be useful to keep supplies organised and if you had concerns about people coming across them you could either buy solid boxes or arrange them in the space in the middle and have your usual under the bed items around them so the boxes were not visible if anyone looked under the bed without getting items out.
    - Chests of Drawers: Most bedrooms have at least one chest of drawers. This could be an opportunity to have a clear out of any unwanted belongings to create storage space, and perhaps either donate unwanted items to charity or sell them to give additional funds for stockpiling. You could fit a worthwhile amount of food in the bottom drawer of even a small bedside cabinet. It's also worth checking to see how much space is underneath the bottom drawer when removed from the chest of drawers to see how much could be concealed in that space.

Bathrooms

You probably wouldn't want to put any food items in the bathroom, but if you can make space for a small storage unit or extra set of shelves, or even room on an existing shelf, this would be an ideal place to store some non food supplies such as soap, toothpaste, shampoos etc.

Loft

If you have a loft, this is a tempting resource in terms of storage but you need to be careful what you place in there. Lofts have extreme temperature fluctuations from very cold in the winter to very warm in summer. Exposing food items (even tins) to these conditions will massively reduce their shelf life and cause them to spoil. For this reason, lofts should not really be used for food items but are a very useful storage space for non food items or equipment (even if unrelated to your stockpiling you could clear out other areas around the house by putting things in the loft to free up more suitable storage space for food elsewhere)

Outside Buildings

If you have a garage or shed, you may wish to look at using these for additional storage. If you want to do this, you need to consider their suitability for this purpose. Some factors to think about are below:

- Security: Are the outbuildings safe and secure so that anything stored within them is not at risk of theft? Can you reinforce the locks / windows etc. to make them harder to get into if somebody did attempt to get in? It would be terrible to create a stockpile which was then stolen if food shortages became so bad that people resorted to theft to feed themselves and their families.

- Can you store items within the building in such a way that they are not visible from the outside? Can you ensure that the building will always be locked?
- Weather and water tight: In a similar way to considering whether you should use a loft or cellar to store food items, you need to assess whether the building provides a suitable environment in which to store your supplies so that they are not at risk of exposure to the elements or extremes of temperature which could cause them to degrade. Garden sheds have no insulation so can get very cold in winter and hot in summer.
- Vermin proof: Outside buildings are far more vulnerable to infestations of vermin, particularly rats and mice. This really is something to be avoided as once you have an infestation it is a major health and hygiene hazard which can be difficult to eradicate once it is established. Attracting rats and mice to a shed would also significantly increase the risk that they would try and get into the house as their population increased. Being overrun with vermin is very bad news indeed so should be avoided at all costs. If you are going to store food items in an outside building, ensure that it is food in containers that vermin cannot get into, these will also help keep the contents dry. Realistically, it is better to store food items in the house if at all possible but sheds and other outbuildings could be a useful receptacle for other items from within the house if you wanted to have a clear out to free up storage space inside.
- Garages: Garages that are attached to the house are a more viable potential storage area as they are more secure, are likely to suffer less temperature fluctuations than a shed at the bottom of your garden and may have

power in them as well as being dry and weather proof. An attached garage with power gives the potential to install shelves or other storage units and perhaps an additional freezer so can be a useful area to store your supplies as long as you are mindful of the risk of attracting rodents and take suitable precautions to prevent this happening and regularly monitor the area to deal with any evidence of rodents appearing in the area before the problem becomes too bad.

Storage Tips
- Don't rely on the freezer or fridge. If the power goes down so do they.
- Don't store everything in the same place.
- Keep supplies out of sight wherever possible.
- Consider the storage requirements of what you are stockpiling- it would be terrible to go to the expense and effort of getting it to find it had deteriorated in storage and was unusable when needed.
- Make sure your storage area is dry and weather proof with minimal temperature fluctuations to preserve the longevity of the supplies stored there.
- Ensure storage areas are vermin proof.
- Remember where you have stored supplies! Easy if most of it is in one place, less easy if it is all over the house. If it is all over the house, consider starting a log of what you have and where you've put it.
- Make sure your storage is secure to minimise the chance of having your supplies stolen.

10- Stretching Your Supplies

If it comes to using your supplies in a food shortage situation, it is worth having a few ideas on how to make them go further if needed. Reading this now may give some ideas on what you could have in your store to help bulk the main food items out if necessary. Being able to bulk out some meals will give you the ability to feed more people or to make your stores last longer should circumstances require. Many meals can be stretched with a few simple additions to make them go much further.

Tinned Soup- you can add lentils or tinned vegetables or beans together with some stock to make a larger, more substantial meal.

Tinned chilli con carne- add some lentils and a tin of beans before cooking until lentils are soft and ready to eat. Add some water if needed. This will significantly increase the amount of food the dish makes.

Mince based dishes: When frying up mince, add a handful of lentils and or some oats. Cook as normal for the dish and once it is ready it will be a larger dish but the additions will be barely noticeable to those eating it. TVP / soya mince is also great to add to mince type dishes to bulk them out.

If you have some tinned vegetables or potatoes, these can be added to many dishes such as soups or curries to bulk them out to make the meal go further.

If you have a meaty meal such as with ham or chicken, keep any leftover meat. Frying it up with whatever vegetables you have around and cooking with stock and the seasoning of your choice will make a nice soup so creating an extra meal. Another way of creating an additional soup meal is if you have a stew type dish then keep any leftovers and add more stock and vegetables to create a stew soup. You may not wish to do this for every meal but if food shortages occur and are severe, being able to create a few extra soup meals would be a useful skill to have.

Baked beans can be bought for as little as £1 for 4 tins from the supermarket bargain ranges. Whilst you may prefer to eat other brands of baked beans as meals, they are useful to have as they are a very cheap way of buying the beans that you can either drain and wash the sauce off before adding to other dishes to bulk them out, or adding spices to create curried or chilli beans so making another dish very cheaply.

Dried mushrooms are useful to have to add to stews, curries, chilli con carne or Bolognese sauces. Add a little extra liquid and they will rehydrate, soaking up the flavours and bulking out the meal.

If water becomes an issue, take care to save any water that tinned food that you use comes in. Whilst it wouldn't be an idea to keep it, if whatever you are cooking has a sauce and needs extra liquid, using the reserved liquid will save you using your precious stored water.

If any foods that you use come packaged in oil (sundried tomatoes are a commonly used one), you can save the oil and use this for cooking with to save using up oil that you have stored.

The ideas above are only a few measures that could be used if food becomes scarce but combined they could allow you to feed a few more people or to eke your supplies out by a few more days which could make all the difference in challenging circumstances.

11- Other Food Sources

Preparing for food shortages by building your own stockpile is sensible, but however much you build up, they will only last a finite amount of time. The hope is that if you need to use them, they will last as long as required as in until food supplies go back to normal again. Unfortunately, in such uncertain times it is impossible to predict how long this could be should food shortages occur.

Therefore, as well as building your own supplies, it would be prudent to consider any ways in which you might be able to access some food supplies whilst food shortages were ongoing. Being able to source some food, even only a small amount of your food requirements, would be good for morale, give variety to your diet and perhaps most importantly mean that your own supplies would last longer if supplemented with other food.

This chapter gives some ideas of alternative sources which it might be possible to access food in times of food shortages and what you might do to improve your chances of accessing it if food shortages occur.

Community Food Growing Schemes

Find out if there is one nearby and if they are looking for volunteers. Even if you are not an expert gardener, if they are looking for volunteers for tasks you can help out with it could be worth joining. If you are an established volunteer / member of the scheme you may have a better chance of qualifying for some of the produce that they grow when food shortages are ongoing.

If food shortages occur, they are likely to be inundated with people wanting to join to get produce that way, so joining beforehand whilst they are still accepting members could be a good investment of time as well as helping a good cause.

Local Vegetable Box Scheme

In a similar vein to the paragraph above- if you can become a customer now, perhaps by setting up a regular order, you will be on their list and an established customer by the time Brexit happens. If food shortages occur at this time, they too are likely to experience a huge surge in demand for their produce. As an existing customer, you will have a better chance of accessing the produce they have available.

As many of these schemes use locally grown produce, there is a good chance that even post Brexit they should be able to supply some food even if it is a restricted range but any additional food coming in during times of food shortage will be worth having. Vegetable box schemes may seem more expensive than supermarket vegetables, but in this situation should be seen as an investment to allow continued access to vegetables after Brexit once supermarket vegetables are severely restricted. If Brexit doesn't happen, or if food shortages don't happen then you can cancel the order if you wish, but until then it is worth considering as a way of ensuring alternative access to food.

Local Meat

If you eat meat, you might want to look into finding another source in case it becomes difficult to get hold of. This may be more possible for those living in rural areas (although some farmers are happy to use courier delivery) but some farmers sell their own produced meat directly to the public. Customers order and pay the farmer who arranges for the meat to be processed before sending it out to customers.

In the same way that joining a local growing scheme or becoming a customer of a vegetable box scheme will hopefully get you on as an existing customer before Brexit, it may be an investment to get on the farmer's customer list before food shortages happen. You would need to check availability and the farmer's policy regarding giving priority to existing customers if they experience high levels of demand but it could be worth looking at for peace of mind.

The quantities of meat are often larger depending on the package ordered (although some farmers may allow you to specify smaller orders) so a freezer will be needed if you wish to do this. You could always split the meat with a friend to make it more affordable and practical to store.

12- Sustainable Food Sources

As well as finding alternative sources of food and supplies to purchase, there are options in terms of securing food on an ongoing basis- from growing it yourself to finding it and catching it.

All options should be considered to see if any appeal to you. If food shortages occur, another potential food source could be a valuable thing to have.

Growing your Own
Growing your own fruit or vegetables or even just herbs can be a way to improve the variety of food that is available to you. If you are living purely on your stockpile while food shortages are ongoing, some fresh fruit or vegetables will be a welcome addition to your diet. If some food is available but the selection is restricted or if prices have risen significantly, home grown fruit and vegetables will again be a welcome addition to allow you to boost your other food stocks and reduce what you need to buy in.

Even if you don't have green fingers, or a large space available to grow plants, it is still possible to grow herbs on your windowsills or tomatoes in pots around the house.

Some of the easiest plants to grow yourself are below:

- o Chard
- o Courgettes
- o Cucumbers
- o French Beans
- o Garlic
- o Jerusalem Artichokes
- o Potatoes
- o Raspberries
- o Rhubarb
- o Rocket
- o Spinach
- o Tomatoes

If you want to grow your own, however much or little, the tips below are worth bearing in mind:

- Whatever the scale of growing you intend to do, the sooner you procure the compost and seeds in order to do so the better in case they become harder to get hold of as Brexit approaches.
- If your growing plans include any outside plants, don't underestimate the time needed to prepare the soil so don't leave this until the last minute.
- If you're a confident gardener, you could consider trying to get an allotment. Keeping an allotment secure if food shortages occur would be a big consideration though.
- If you're an experienced gardener but have very limited space, see if there are any friends or neighbours nearby with large enough gardens not to mind you using some of theirs in return for some of the crops you grow.

- If you're growing crops in the garden, think about planting them around the area rather than in one "vegetable area" in order to make them less noticeable to people who visit or pass the garden.
- Choose your plants carefully. The easier they are to grow the better. Some of the easiest crops to grow are Chard, Courgettes, Cucumbers, French Beans, Garlic, Jerusalem Artichokes (keep them in a pot though or they'll take over your garden), Raspberries and Rocket. Some need to be planted months before, and some need more help than others but they are easy to grow. If you can grow some potatoes as well that will give a great boost to your supplies.
- Whether you're a total novice at gardening or want to know how to do it with limited space available, there are many books available on eBay or Amazon at next to nothing so purchasing one would be a worthwhile investment.

Chickens

Chickens are a lovely way to get a supply of fresh eggs (and potentially meat too but this isn't for the faint hearted). However, they come with their own issues which need considering before you get them- they shouldn't be bought on a whim.

- Are you allowed to keep them? Many houses have restrictions on the deeds which state chickens can't be kept there. Whether anyone will care about this once Brexit hits is debatable but it's wise to check before you get them so you can make an informed decision about whether you want to go ahead should your deeds state they can't be kept at your property.

- You'll need to feed them. Obvious but if you're prepping for your family members that will need to include the chickens. Individually, they eat approximately 100-150g of feed a day which is a small amount but multiplying that by the number of chickens and then by the number of days of food you want stored up for them and you might find this is a significant amount of feed. Corn may well become more difficult or expensive to get due to the weather conditions causing problems to farmers. Storing feed must be done correctly in order to keep it dry so it doesn't get damp (and risk going mouldy and therefore unusable) and in vermin proof containers (metal bins work well) to prevent rodents moving in. A rodent infestation is something to be avoided at all costs.
- Chickens love scraps and leftovers. Whilst it is technically illegal to feed these to them, whether this is an issue post Brexit remains to be seen. Many chicken owners already disregard this and feed them leftovers which can supplement their diet, but remember if food shortages occur there will be less scraps and leftovers to give to them.
- Safety and security of your chickens could be an issue. If food shortages hit, then all food sources will be a target for theft. You should consider how to keep the chickens secure and ideally so that people around you don't realise you have them. Don't keep a cockerel as they are very noisy (although if you wanted to breed them for meat you would need one), but hens make some noise too.

- Chickens are lovely but need daily attention, require quite a lot of cleaning out and keepers need some knowledge of how to keep them healthy and happy. If you want chickens, check out websites and books for novice chicken keepers to check you can meet their needs and are able to make the commitment to look after them properly.
- Also remember that they usually stop laying in winter so having them doesn't guarantee eggs all year around. That said, they are wonderful characters and great fun to have around if your circumstances allow.

Foraging

Foraging is the practice of gathering wild food for free. It can yield a surprising amount of food if you know what you're looking for, even in the UK. Some foods should be eaten straightaway, others lend themselves to preserving if you find a glut of them.

A brief list of what is out there to forage and when they are available is below:

Season	Food	Use
Spring	Dandelion	Leaves in Salads
Spring	Wild Watercress	Salads and Soups
Spring	Hawthorn Leaves	Salads
Spring / Summer	Nettles	Soups
Spring / Summer	Wild Garlic	Salads, Soups, Cooking with anything that uses Garlic. Pesto.

Season	Food	Use
Summer	Chickweed	Salads or make into Pesto.
Summer	Elderflowers	Cordial
Summer	Ground elder	An invasive weed but edible too. Fry or steam the leaves as vegetable side or use in soups / stews.
Summer / Autumn	Raspberries	Eat as fruit, use in desserts, preserve as jam, freeze.
Autumn	Beechnuts	Eat as snacks or roast to use in similar way to pine nuts. Don't eat too many.
Autumn	Bilberries	Eat as fruit, use in desserts, preserve in jam, freeze.
Autumn	Blackberries (Brambles)	Eat as fruit, use in desserts, preserve in jam, freeze. Great source of Vitamin C.
Autumn	Elderberries	Use in desserts (great in crumbles), make syrups, preserve in jam. Freeze. Great source of Vitamin C.
Autumn	Hazelnuts	Eat as snack, roast, Hazelnut Butter.
Autumn	Rosehips	Great source of Vitamin C. Used to make syrup in World War 2 to replace citrus fruit imports. Also make jellies or preserve as jam.
Autumn / Winter	Bullace	Make jams, preserves, fruit wine and liqueurs.

Season	Food	Use
Autumn / Winter	Sweet Chestnuts	Cook then eat as snacks. Also use as stuffing or desserts.
Winter	Acorns	Don't eat raw! Boil then roast and eat as snacks. Can make Acorn flour.
Winter	Pine nuts	From pine cones. Roast and use for salads, pesto, snacking.

This is just a selection of the plants that can be foraged in the UK throughout the year.

If you live by the sea, you may also be able to get hold of Sea Beet which is like Chard as well as seaweed which is edible too.

The UK also has many wild mushrooms and fungi that can be foraged. The trouble with wild mushrooms is that the UK also has plenty of highly poisonous mushrooms and it is not always easy to differentiate between poisonous and edible. If you want to try mushroom foraging, it is best to go with an expert who can identify the different types for you. You can purchase books with detailed illustrations to refer to on foraging trips but it is safest to try to go with an expert the first few times.

See if there are any local foraging groups or excursions anywhere local to you and go along- it is more fun and informative to go the first time with people who can point out what is edible- mushrooms and everything else and this will give you confidence to try again in the future.

You can purchase foraging journals which are useful as you can keep a record of the trips you make with what you found, where you found it and when enabling you to build a record of the best places and times to forage in your own area.

Foraging is definitely a worthwhile activity to do if you are able as you can secure a great selection of foods throughout the year.

<u>Fishing</u>
If you are good at fishing then that could be a very useful skill to have. Whether it is fishing in rivers or in the sea, don't underestimate its possible value in supplementing your food supplies.

If you intend to fish for food, make sure your equipment is all in good working order and any replacement bits bought sooner rather than later just in case.

When fishing don't forget to take basic precautions in terms of safety- always tell someone where you are going and when you will be back so that the alarm can be raised if you don't get back in time. Make sure you wear a lifejacket if going out in a boat and that the boat is seaworthy and you know what you are doing with it. No amount of fish is worth having an accident at sea or on the river which could be fatal.

As well as traditional fishing with a line, another option if you live near the sea could be crabbing with line and a bait off a pier or similar. It is also possible to purchase lobster pot type fishing nets from Amazon and eBay. Although these may seem a bit like cheating, they may allow you to catch more fish than you would otherwise and possibly get different seafood such as a lobster if you got really lucky. As for all fishing, if using these take all sensible precautions in order to maintain your safety which must be the priority.

Hunting

This will only be an option for a few people, but for those with the knowledge, equipment and ability to do it, hunting is another way to get food. Rabbits and birds such as pheasants are hunted anyway (pheasants only exist in the numbers they do as they are reared and fed for the sporting shooting industry). Don't hunt unless you know what you are doing, it could be very dangerous.

Hunting is included here as a reminder that it is an option- whilst you may not be able to do it others will so if things get very tough it may be possible to buy hunted meat from those who do.

Bartering

This is the exchange of goods or services for other goods or services rather than money changing hands. Potentially a great way to get your hands on items you need if you have a skill or surplus of another resource.

Caution should be used if contemplating bartering though- the last thing you want is for it to become known that you have got stocks sufficient that you have spare to barter with. For this reason you should be very careful, perhaps either only swap skills or services (perhaps you're a great sewer or can offer help with gardening or childcare etc.) for food or other items or services that you need so nobody finds out you have your own supplies.

Swapping skills for skills will not directly get you more food but it may save you money which you can then use to purchase what you need if available.

13- Babies and Young Children

If you have a baby or young child, it is vitally important to ensure that you have everything that is required to meet their needs for the amount of time you are preparing for. They are smaller so more vulnerable to missing food or becoming poorly. They are too young to understand what is happening so are likely to become more distressed if something they need is missing than an adult or older child who could understand the situation better.

It could be worth setting aside a separate section of your stockpile for baby or child items- this way it will be easier to see at a glance what you need (and therefore what you still need to get). If you are record keeping, you could also set up a specific section for baby items to keep a close eye on what stores you have and still need.

Items that could be necessary for babies or young children depending on their age include:
- Nappies (make sure you regularly change them as your child grows to ensure you have the right size "in stock"). If you don't use disposable nappies, still consider having a few- they are always good for emergencies. If power and water became an issue and you couldn't wash cotton nappies that would be a real problem if you ran out so it could be useful to have a few disposables stored away as a back up option.
- Nappy sacks- to dispose of the nappies in and maintain hygiene.

- Wipes (the sort you usually use on your child- trading down is usually fine but for baby wipes it is safest to go with what works i.e. not running the risk that the baby develops a rash to a new sort of wipe when there are no alternatives available)
- Sudacrem / nappy cream- just in case nappy rash happens. If it isn't something your child usually gets you could chance it with a small tub but remember they can get it as their diet changes or if they are teething so even if they don't have it now it's safest to have a nappy rash treatment just in case.
- Bonjela / teething gel / teething granules- teething is difficult for all concerned. Make sure you have stocks of whatever you have found works for your child (or perhaps a couple of options if your baby hasn't started teething yet).
- Medicine suitable for your baby / child- Calpol, Ibuprofen etc. Make sure you understand how the doses work if you don't use it often. If your child gets poorly, there's nothing worse than finding you've run out of Calpol and that's without potentially being in a time where the shops are empty. Don't take the risk and have some stashed away.
- Formula- Ideally a tub of the powder and some of the long life premade bottles of formula that many brands do these days. You will need to regularly review the formula you have "in stock" as shelf life isn't always as long as you'd like, and to ensure that you have the right "stage" of formula milk that your baby is on in the stockpile.

- If your baby is currently breastfed, formula is not quite so much of a concern but for peace of mind it could be sensible to have at least some formula for the baby as a contingency- just in case breastfeeding has to stop suddenly for example if baby's Mum becomes ill and unable to breastfeed. If you are storing it as a contingency and not yet using it, make sure you have a couple of bottles to go with it and the necessary equipment to sterilize the bottles. This may sound like overkill but many people would rather store these items than risk having a hungry baby with no formula available.

- Baby food- if your baby is very young and might start weaning round about Brexit time it's worth thinking about this. Some people like jars (check the dates), others start on baby rice and pureed vegetables. Having some baby rice stored away and either some vegetables you plan to puree frozen or tinned so you can make up the baby food from existing supplies would give peace of mind. Make sure you have the necessary spoons and other baby feeding paraphernalia to go with the food. If your child is older and on any form of bought baby food, you may wish to have some of that stored away. Whatever you plan to feed your child, have some stored away just in case. With proper stock rotation and planning, this won't be wasted as you use it but will ensure you have sufficient stocks should they be needed.

14-Pets

Pets are members of the family and therefore you should prep for them too. This task will be easy if you have one small dog or cat in terms of what you need to store away, less so if you have a few pets especially if they are big ones. The sooner you start thinking about this the better as most pet food has a good shelf life so you can start storing this well in advance, and depending on the size of your menagerie you may need a large quantity of it.

As with the rest of your stockpile, use stock rotation to ensure that you are always storing the food with the longest shelf life.

Consider trading down if your pets are on a premium food. Tinned food can have huge variations in price and if you're buying a month or more of food this can make a big difference to the total cost. Consider buying a selection of different pet foods at different prices to see if your pet will eat any of the cheaper ones (you don't want to run the risk of it not eating the food you've got stored away when it's the only food available).

Trading down now would give reassurance that the pet will eat it, and the money saved could be put towards buying more for the stockpile. If your pet won't eat cheaper food, or if you feel it is necessary to remain on the food it eats now for health reasons (some dogs and cats have specific dietary needs and can't easily have their diet changed, especially those with allergies or on special vet food for a medical condition) then you will need to accept that you are going to need to buy more of it to ensure you have a suitable amount stored away.

This applies to animals fed on kibble / dried diets too. Feeders of these diets should be sure to check the best before dates of the food they store as kibble has a shorter shelf life than tinned food. It is very important to store the food in a secure container to prevent it being got at by rodents (or depending on where you put it, the pet it is for!).

If you feed a raw diet, then you can stock the freezer with more raw food fairly easily if you have spare freezer space available, but the risk here is that the power goes down for long enough that the freezer thaws fully and the food is spoiled. Raw feeding pet owners may want to consider some sort of back-up food that they would be willing to feed if the raw food was lost or used up.

Whatever pet you have, work out how much food it will need for the time period you are prepping for and then ensure you have this amount in your store. For dogs and cats and small fluffy creatures this is easy enough to work out and do. If you have more exotic pets this may be more complicated but still needs to be done.

If you have lizards or other animals living in vivariums, or heated tanks, you need to have a plan in case the power goes down to keep them warm for as long as possible. Put a duvet or thick blanket around the tank to insulate the heat and that should keep it warm for a while.

If you have a fish tank and are worried that they have insufficient oxygen as a short term measure you can put some tank water into a clean bottle, seal it and shake vigorously. Then replace the water into the tank and this will at least improve the situation a little and hopefully keep them going until the power goes back on. Don't forget to buy extra fish food for them too.

Items you should have stored for your pet could include:
- Enough food
- For dogs, poo bags.
- Medication – flea and worming treatment (be vigilant with use by dates on these- it can be very dangerous to the pet to use them once the date has expired as they can become poisonous).
- For cats- Cat litter.
- For cage or tank living animals- whatever bedding / litter they have so that they can be cleaned out as usual.
- If a pet has a chronic health condition for which it needs regular medication, look at stockpiling more of it. Ironically it may prove easier to stockpile medication for your pets than it is for yourself.
- Any supplements or vitamins your pet needs.

It's difficult to give an exhaustive list as there are so many different pets! Essentially, plan what your pet needs – food and otherwise and work this into your stockpiling plans. Purchasing so much extra pet food is likely to be quite expensive so if your animal isn't on a specific diet or a fussy eater, you could look at signing up to some of these companies who will send out free samples or highly discounted food as a subsidized trial as a way to boost your stocks quickly.

15- Useful Equipment

As well as prepping by creating stockpiles of food and non food consumables, there are some items of equipment that you should consider getting. Some are pretty much essential whether you are prepping for three days or three months, others are desirable but you can live without them. Some of these are mentioned in previous chapters, but more detail is given here.

<u>Tin Openers!!</u> Don't forget these- at least two even if you have one already. If you're buying lots of tins you don't want to find you don't have a tin opener and buying two means if one breaks or gets mislaid you have another in reserve.

<u>Lighting</u>

- Torches- preferably a selection and with plenty of spare batteries. An ideal selection would be at least one high powered one, a head torch and a few small cheaper ones to keep around the house (for example in the bathroom to avoid anyone getting plunged into darkness when there is a power cut). If you are getting a few, it's useful to have one in the kitchen too- the smaller ones can be hung up discreetly from a hook behind the curtains or similar and ensure all family members know where they are. Start off with a couple of torches say a high powered one and another and add to the collection over time, remembering to add more batteries as you add more torches.

- If you have a spare head torch in a power cut, fill a 4 pint plastic milk container with water and attach the head torch to the outside of the container so that the light is pointing in towards the water, it creates a really effective glowing effect through the water.
- LED lights- wind up or battery powered (but make sure you have plenty of batteries). Nice way to create light in a room which is more like having an actual light rather than a torch. These can be bought for reasonable prices so worth getting at least one if you can.
- Candles and matches / lighters (or both). **If you want to use candles, please be vigilant about using them safely particularly if you have children or other family members (or pets) who might knock them over.** Get candles as well as not instead of torches. Candles can be handy in terms of heat- a couple of tea lights under an upside down terracotta flowerpot can add some extra heat to a cold room.
- Glowsticks / lightsticks- these can be bought fairly cheaply online. Not a replacement for torches or LED lights but potentially a useful addition. Single use- click to activate and they are light for a few hours. It's possible to put one in a pint size plastic milk container filled with water to create more of a glowing effect.

Power

Hopefully there won't be any issues with power other than the usual we get as a result of weather in the UK, but since we don't know what will happen it is sensible to look at how to prepare in case of more serious problems with power post Brexit. Any power related preparations will also be useful if we have normal weather related power cuts.

- Lots of batteries. Make sure you have batteries for all the battery powered items you would use in a power cut. If you have different types of torches make sure you have batteries suitable for all of them. Rechargeable batteries are good but remember they need recharging- if it is a short power cut and you always have some charged batteries around this will be fine but if the power cut goes on for longer you don't want to be stuck without a way to recharge. If you use rechargeable batteries, make sure you always recharge them when used and consider having at least a few normal batteries in your supplies as a reserve.
- Power banks- these are like big rechargeable batteries that you can plug your phone (or if the power bank has enough capacity your tablet) in to charge. Keeping phones charged and usable is important but remember you need to ensure the power bank is properly charged at all times. Check out Amazon for realistic prices for the different capacities as the prices they sell at can vary widely and you don't want to pay too much for one.
- Solar powered chargers / power banks- these are useful, particularly if needed in better weather when they can recharge. Check the reviews for these products carefully as there can be a wide variation between item quality and reliability as well as price. A good one can be invaluable so definitely worth looking into.

- Generators: A drastic option! Not one this book will attempt to look at in any detail other than to say if you are considering getting one:
  - Do you know how to operate it and keep it going?
  - What will you do about storing fuel for it
  - Where do you live? Running a generator in the middle of a built up area is going to create noticeable noise that could outweigh any benefits brought by the electricity gained by making you an obvious target as someone who has a generator and presumably other resources that those nearby may wish to obtain.
  - If you live in the middle of nowhere with nobody nearby to hear it running, it may be a more viable option.
  - Where will you put it to ensure no problems with the fumes it creates?

  If you are interested in generators, please do thorough specialist research before getting one.

Methods of heating food with no power

It would be sensible to have a way of heating your food if the power goes off. When we have a power cut, we don't know how long it will last. Even a short power cut can make things difficult in terms of food preparation and general day to day life so having equipment to enable you to continue living as normally as possible is desirable if resources allow.

Main priority as you research this is to be sure you can use the equipment you have safely. Consider how you will make sure it is safe so family members don't get burned / knock it over etc. Also consider any fumes it will emit in terms of where you can use it safely. Follow the manufacturers' instructions when using them as well as plenty of common sense. With young or vulnerable family members, keep it somewhere that they can't access it on their own. Make sure you have carbon monoxide monitors and smoke alarms in the house and regularly check that they are still working. Being able to cook is important but not as important as avoiding injury so use caution at all times!

Camping Stoves
- Camping stoves are small so easy to store and cheap to buy. They often come in a nice set with fuel tablets and a mess tin (or you can make a set up yourself). The downside of their size is that they may struggle to heat larger volumes of food (if you are cooking for more than a couple of people), but you could always consider getting two if you have a larger household to look after. They are so easy to use and convenient, they are worth having. Use them outside.
- Camping stoves can be picked up very cheaply at end of season sales from Millets or similar, also a wide range available on Amazon.
- Consider getting a few accessories to go with your camping stove- a couple of mess tins that you can cook in and eat out of as well as a camping kettle as these are designed to be used with camping stoves and safer than boiling water in a pan on a stove.

- Whatever fuel your stove uses, make sure you buy plenty of it so that you don't worry about using it due to dwindling fuel supplies.

Cobb Barbeque

Cobb Barbeques are not a cheap item of kit, but they are popular so you may already have one. If this is the case, don't forget about it as they are a very useful gadget for cooking larger amounts of food than a camping stove, and you can even roast a whole chicken in one. If you don't have one, check them out and consider trying to get one when circumstances allow. It is always worth keeping an eye out on eBay to see if any second hand ones pop up there at a bargain price. As for camping stoves, if you have one make sure you have plenty of fuel for it- it is often heavily discounted going into winter.

Keeping Warm
- Brexit will happen in spring so hopefully the worst of the winter weather will be gone, but there is still the possibility of a cold snap. Hopefully any power related post Brexit problems would have been resolved by the time winter comes round again, but it is as well to be prepared and power cuts can happen for many reasons.
- If it gets very cold, you are better trying to heat one room well and everyone living in there (if this will work for your family) until the power comes on. It is easier and more effective to heat one room than the whole house. Ensure the door is kept shut to keep the heat in the room, keep the curtains shut to stop heat escaping and that will be a good start to at least having one warm room.

- If you have an open fire, this is a good way to keep warm in a power cut (but think about whether you think people seeing the smoke is a risk). If you plan to use your open fire, ensure that you know how to use it, have sufficient safety equipment such as a fire guard to stop younger or vulnerable family members getting too close to it. Do not use your fire until it has been swept by a professional chimney sweep and confirmed safe to use. Fuel is widely available- either bought or you could use wood but be sure to check the regulations in your local area as some are quite strict in terms of what people there are allowed to burn in home fires.
- As already mentioned, flower pot heaters can help take the chill off a room as the heat from the candles heats up the terracotta pot which then warms the room. Make sure you know how to use it properly (you might need more than one) and that you have ensured that family members are not at risk of hurting themselves or knocking it over with the accompanying fire risk.
- Putting bubble wrap on the inside of your windows can improve their insulation which will make your room warmer. This is easy to do, and the bubble wrap is easily removed afterwards so worth considering if it is an option for you and having some bubble wrap in the house if you think it is.
- Ensure you have plenty of blankets to sit under.
- Wearing multiple thinner layers is more effective than one thick one in terms of keeping you warm. Make sure that family members have a few layers to put on and if it gets really cold, wearing a warm hat will help too.
- Ensure you have the equipment and supplies needed to make warm drinks for your family.

Communication

Hopefully things won't get so bad that mobile phones no longer work. However, if you want to think of all problems that could occur it is worth thinking about what you and your family would do if mobiles didn't work. Mobiles are fantastic but they are dependent on a complex system to keep them going, and if any of these go down so do the phones in that area. Those living in rural areas are likely to have experienced the inconvenience of their mobile not getting a signal when the local mast goes down either for maintenance or due to storm or weather damage. Consider how you would manage communication with family members who were out and about if mobile phones stopped working for any length of time. One solution could be hand held or CB radios. CB radios used to be very popular as a means of communication, and hand-held radios (walkie talkies) could be useful if you are out and about.

The author's family has a set of walkie talkies just in case, if needed they can be used as an alternative form of communication if anybody needs to go out for any reason and the mobiles are down. Modern walkie talkies have an impressive range and radio communication in general has moved on in recent years. Unfortunately, they are quite expensive, but worth looking at if you are worried about loss of communication should mobiles go down for any reason. If you are interested in CB radios, look into this further for more information on the most suitable ones to purchase for a beginner and also around the licensing requirements to own and operate one. The big advantage of a CB radio is that potentially you can use them to communicate with people all over the world, and some people enjoy doing this as a hobby.

Also consider your landline telephone- many don't work if there is a power cut, some that plug directly into the phone line do and are inexpensive to buy. If you are worried about power cuts you may wish to consider purchasing a handset that will work when the power is down.

Getting Around

Stockpiling fuel for vehicles is not generally a good idea. It is illegal to have more than a small amount stored, it does not last well so can go off pretty quickly and is a huge fire risk if stored incorrectly.

The safest, most sensible way to go about making sure you have fuel in your car is to make sure you just always have more fuel in your tank at any time. Rather than going to the garage when the car gets to below a quarter of a tank, change your habits so that you fill up when it gets to a half or even three quarters full. This way you will always have a good few miles worth of fuel in the car, you'll be using it all the time so it won't go off and you won't have the worry of trying to store it safely. If fuel shortages occur, half a tank or more of fuel should still last most people a reasonable amount of time if they are careful.

You can't prep to have months' worth of fuel just in case, if you aim to ensure that you always have a few days' worth hopefully this will be enough to tide you over through any short term fuel shortages.

Think about how you could save fuel if fuel availability became an issue. Could you reduce your journeys in some way? Car share to reduce the amount of fuel used? Take alternative transport (public transport, cycling, walking) for some journeys at least? Try to think about how you could do this before you have to so that you have a plan of action should the need arise.

16- Morale

Maintaining the good morale of your family is important. If food shortages occur, then it is going to be a pretty miserable time however long it goes on for as that is likely to be one of many problems rather than just one. If you can keep your family's morale good then that will make difficult times much easier to live through.

Think about how you could prepare for this in advance. Is there a particular food that each family member likes that you could have stored away to bring out for occasional treats? Do family members have a particular activity such as board game or craft activity they like to do that you could have the necessary materials for?

Some ideas for what you could store are below:

Favourite Meals
Why not store the supplies needed to make each family member's favourite meal. Ask them what it is if needed. The author's family favourites are:

- Sausages, mash, gravy, peas
- Cheesy pasta
- Pizza
- Spaghetti Bolognese
- Tuna pasta bake

Fortunately, these are all pretty straightforward meals to make from the store cupboard but if yours are less so then consider how you can adapt them to come up with something similar. Having a few meals worth of each is a good way to make sure you can rustle up a favourite meal to boost morale- everyone likes their favourite meal from time to time and it will give a nice sense of normality to the whole family.

Treats

In a similar way to storing the makings of everyone's favourite meal, you could do the same with everyone's favourite chocolate bar or similar (if they don't like chocolate). Most chocolate has a pretty good shelf life so most should be storable at least for a few months (remember stock rotation). Also remember not to let other family members know about this part of your prepping at least or you run the risk of them helping themselves too early.

Other high value occasional treats could include the makings of a cake if you like baking, chocolate spreads if your family like these, tinned puddings to have from time to time.

Vices

If someone in the family likes a glass of wine or other tipple, if resources allow putting a couple of bottles / drinks' worth in your stores could allow the occasional treat for them.

If anyone smokes, you may not want to stock up on cigarettes (for cost reasons apart from anything else) but perhaps some nicotine replacement products which can be bought fairly cheaply in case they run out of cigarettes could come in very handy for the whole family rather than having a nicotine deprived family member adding to an already stressful situation.

Activities

Consider what activities your family likes to do. If things get difficult, it may be better for everyone to stay inside for a couple of days to ride any local problems out rather than braving the shops or populated areas in the midst of largescale panic buying or other heated situations. Even if we don't have power issues, you may not want everyone watching television or on the internet all day so having some alternative activities ready could be helpful to everyone. Many of the suggested items below can be bought very cheaply either online or in discount or charity shops.

- Crafts- knitting, sewing, embroidery etc. If anyone likes doing this consider having some materials available if required.
- Painting / Drawing- a pad of paper and a set of paints / pencils / felt tips.
- Colouring Books- can be bought very cheaply at pound shops or similar for either adult colouring or if you have any younger family members.
- Reading- a selection of books that nobody has read in a style / subject that you know they like
- Jigsaws / Board Games- a great way to pass time if your family enjoys them and good for family time too as everyone can take part.

These may seem a strange thing to add to your preparations but if the need arises, they could be very beneficial to your family's morale and therefore wellbeing and can be assembled at little cost and stored around the house.

17- Grab Bags

This book is about preparing to make sure you have everything you need in the house to deal with potential food shortages. However, no book about prepping would be complete without at least introducing the concept of Grab Bags.

Grab Bags are bags that you have ready packed (as in you just need to grab them when needed) in case there is an emergency which means you and your family need to leave your home with little or no notice.

Most preppers will have a Grab Bag, particularly those that live in countries that tend to have serious natural disasters that require emergency evacuation from home such as floods and earthquakes. Grab Bags are becoming more commonly used in the UK, with areas prone to flooding encouraging residents to have them just in case.

Grab Bags should contain essentials to last a household three days- such as clothes, food and important documents as well as additional equipment such as torches, personal medication and phone chargers. Grab Bags should include essentials for the whole family.

Grab Bags are worth having as they give peace of mind that should an emergency such as fire or flood occur, and you have to leave home immediately, at least you will have some essentials to get you through the first few days.

Items to put in a Grab Bag include:

- Basic First Aid kit (you can get them on eBay / Amazon)
- Copies of important documents- passports, birth certificates, marriage certificate, driving licence, something with your National Insurance number on plus details of your house and car insurances such as policy numbers. You could laminate them or store them in a sealed plastic bag or wallet to protect them. These will be helpful if you need to prove your identity or start the process of an insurance claim if there has been any damage to your property.
- Any prescription drugs you rely upon (you would need to be careful to rotate these regularly to ensure the medication in the Grab Bag at any time is in date).
- Cash and credit cards
- Spare car keys
- Toiletries and hygiene products as required (toothpaste, spare toothbrush, sanitary products etc.)
- Spare mobile phone charger and power bank (keep charged so check and charge regularly)
- Items that particular family members rely on- for example nappies and wipes if you have a baby or young child and formula if you use this.
- Spare clothes for three days. If space becomes an issue you may not wish to pack three new outfits but underwear and a change of trousers / top and a warm jumper would be a sensible minimum.
- Torch and spare batteries.
- Wind up radio.
- Bottled water and emergency food to last three days.
- Spare set of house keys.

- Copy of your family's Emergency Plan (covered in its own chapter later on in the book)

Obviously, this is an extensive list, and if you have more than one or two people in your household is going to be a significant amount to carry. A spare suitcase rather than a bag is worth considering if you are concerned about the volume of what you put together as your Grab Bag contents.

Once you have your Grab Bag complete, you need to ensure it is kept in a place where it is easy to get to in a hurry. This could be the cupboard under the stairs or if you have a utility room or similar perhaps it could go in there. The important things are that it needs to be easily accessible, and everyone in the family needs to know where it is if needed.

Make sure you review the contents of your Grab Bag regularly- at least twice a year, every three months would be better. This would be to check that battery packs are charged (if not charge them), medication is in date, and in the case of children that the clothes packed for them still fit and haven't been outgrown. You can also take account of seasons and change the packed clothes accordingly, or just pack clothes that are versatile enough to do for most weather conditions in your area. In terms of putting enough clothes away into the Grab Bag, this can be done cheaply if needed. Either use old clothes (that still fit) or if you want to buy additional clothes for this purpose cheap clothes can be found in charity shops or on eBay.

If your household is more than one or two people, considering having more than one bag. If you have children, they could have a bag and the adults could have a bag. This could give more capacity for clothes, nappies and everything else you need to have but make sure however many bags you set up, they are all in an accessible place and that everyone knows where they are (and if more than one bag, how many there should be to take with you) if you have to leave quickly.

If you have pets, you should create a small Emergency Bag for them too. Some pet food, a blanket they are familiar with (so it smells of home), copy of their vaccination certificate and food / water bowls. If you have a cat, keep a cat travel basket around to put it in if you need to leave home quickly. If you have a dog, consider adding a spare lead and bags to clear up after them when you've walked them.

Emergency Bag

As well as a Grab Bag for the house, it is sensible to have an Emergency Bag to keep in your car. This is probably the most commonly done prepping, even though people may not think of it as that, because they are told to by the motoring organisations in the winter.

Items you could include in your Emergency Bag for the car are listed below.
- Warm blanket (you can get picnic ones that fold down very small) or sleeping bag (get one that folds into its own little bag for ease of storage in the car)
- Foil blanket
- High calorie snacks such as chocolate or biscuits or Kendal Mint Cake

- Water (beware of it freezing in the winter- consider squeezing some of the air out and resealing if it is very cold)
- Phone charger and power bank (you can charge off your car if it's running but if you break down somewhere and the car is dead then you'll need the power bank). You can get chargers that run off normal AA batteries too.
- Towel- in case you get wet. You can get compressed ones very cheaply that are tiny to store but open up once the package is opened.
- Warm clothes- minimum of a warm jumper and an extra pair of socks.
- Waterproof jacket (even a Pac a Mac type one so it is small to store is better than nothing in case you end up stranded somewhere on a wet night and have to get out of the car although a warmer one would be better but probably bulkier)
- Folding shovel (in case you're stuck in the snow)
- Warm gloves and a hat (these can be bought very cheaply as an extra set to keep in the car)
- First Aid Kit- even a small basic one that you can get easily from eBay / Amazon. It's nice to get a set as then it all comes in its own little pouch but they usually have room to add a few more items if you wish.
- Torch and spare batteries.
- Handwarmers (the sort that you click the disc in the middle and it sets off a reaction to make it warm). These are cheap so more than one if you have room as if you need one you probably need two. They are reusable.
- Pen and small notebook

- Small LED light- wind up or battery powered. You could also add a couple of the light sticks that can be purchased cheaply for additional light options (rather than risk being stuck out on your own in the dark somewhere)
- Self heating hot drinks- you can purchase drinks that are packaged in such a way that once activated the drink warms up to give you a warm drink. Flavour options include coffee and hot chocolate. They are on the expensive side but if you can include one and were ever stuck out in the cold, you'd be glad of it. They do have a long shelf life.
- MRE rations- these are designed for military use so for soldiers out in the wild to eat. They are also quite expensive but you can purchase individual components as well as the whole 24 hour pack and again if you got in the situation where you were stuck somewhere you would be glad you had them.
- Jump leads
- Warning triangle
- Tow rope

Many of the items listed are similar to those you might have in your home or Grab Bag. Don't worry about duplication- better to have more than one of an item to make sure you always have one where you are when you need it. In an emergency you could take one from one store (as in from the car to use in the house) although it is very important to make sure it is replaced immediately. You don't want to go to use an item that should be in a store to find it is missing as someone has "borrowed" it but it is useful to have backups of some items in case of an emergency.

18- Emergency Plan

Emergencies can take many forms. An Emergency Plan is a straightforward piece of prepping and can help in many different types of emergencies.

The Emergency Plan is a document you create for you and your family which gives information that is likely to be useful if an emergency occurs. As well as putting contact details for all family members and their places of work (or school / childcare), it also outlines what family members should do if an emergency occurs. Every member of the family should have one. If it is just one or two sides of a single piece of paper, it should easily fit into most purses or wallets if folded.

Information you could put into your Emergency Plan includes:

- Contact details for all family members (mobile phone, landline, work, school, childcare provider)
- Contact details for organisations you may need to contact in an emergency:
  - Doctor
  - Vet
  - Dentist
  - Hospital
  - Insurance companies
- Details of insurance policies- as well as the phone numbers, the policy numbers and details for what each policy covers e.g. have a heading for House and the policy number and insurance contact details and the same for any vehicles you have.

- Emergency meeting place: If an emergency that meant you had to leave your home occurred, where would you and any family members meet up? Identify a suitable location and record it in the plan.
- Emergency place to stay (local) - have you a friend or other family member living locally you could all stay with if something happened that meant you had to leave your home? Find out if anyone locally would allow you all to stay in an emergency and record their name and contact details in the Emergency Plan. Far better to have made this arrangement on a hypothetical basis in advance than have something happen and then be panicking about the emergency and having to find somewhere for you all to stay. Make sure everyone knows the address and how to get there as well as the person's contact details.
- Emergency place to stay (out of area)- As well as having someone you could stay with in an emergency in the local area, you may wish to make arrangements for somewhere / someone to with stay further away in case there was an emergency that meant people were asked to leave the immediate area. Again, unlikely as it may be, if something did happen that meant your family had to leave the immediate area it would be reassuring to know you had somewhere else to go without frantically ringing round friends and family and hotels to find somewhere to go. Make sure everyone knows the address and how to get there as well as the person's contact details.

- Make plans for different emergencies ranging from if one of the adults in the family has to go into hospital or is otherwise unable to collect children from school / childcare- do you have anyone you could contact who would be willing to do this? Put their contact details in the plan. You could call it something like "Back Up Kids Pick Up" or similar to make it clear what it is. Go through possible emergencies that could happen to your household and again make a plan and put relevant contact details in so everyone knows what should happen if an emergency does occur. This way if something happens, whether it is the car breaking down so you can't collect the kids, or the whole town floods and you all have to leave immediately you will have a plan and a place to go with contact numbers for the people you need to contact already available. This will make dealing with whatever emergency has happened that little bit easier.

Remind family members that in case of a widespread emergency, it is better to communicate via text than try to make a call- texts are more likely to get through.

19- A Few Food Ideas

When you are doing your planning, it is a good idea to identify meals that you and your family like and that can be made from stockpile ingredients. This can seem a daunting task when you first start, so this chapter gives a few meal ideas. Either use these as the starting point for your planning, or if these particular meals aren't ones that you would make then they can at least be inspiration as to the type of meals you could plan for.

There are three sections: Soups, Mains and Puddings. Each food idea has the necessary ingredients as well as brief instructions on how to make it. The ingredients are left deliberately vague as obviously quantities will vary depending on how many people you will be making the food for, but the information is sufficient to give ideas and a starting point for cooking each dish. Some are more assembly jobs than cooking but again, are included to give ideas on what can be stored to produce different meals. You may not want to make a pudding for every meal, but the occasional pudding will be a great morale booster for many families so are included here for that reason.

For further ideas, there are plenty of books and websites which give ideas for store cupboard cooking.

Note- recipes state olive oil as this is the author's preference however vegetable or sunflower oil would do just as well if you prefer, or even ghee if you are out of oil.

Soups

Although Brexit will happen in Spring, when people may eat less soup, it is still a versatile and quick form of food to be able to make so it is worth planning to be able to make at least a few soups. Soups are good as they can be bulked up to make a heartier dish. They can be rustled up quickly and you can also use different flavours to make various different types of food to try and maintain a varied diet.

Chicken Noodle Soup

A great store cupboard dish- only a few ingredients, dead easy to make and a nice warming soup.

Ingredients
- o Tinned chicken (or fresh if you have it)
- o Tin of sweetcorn (drained)
- o Chicken or Vegetable Stock cube.
- o Handful of dried spaghetti broken into small pieces
- o Teaspoon of oil
- o Hot water

Instructions

Finely chop up the tinned chicken (you could even use a little saved from a tin used for another dish). Heat a pan with the teaspoon of oil. Gently fry the chicken pieces and sweetcorn for a moment before adding the hot water. Dissolve the stock cube into the pan and then add the broken up spaghetti. Bring to the boil and then simmer for as long as it takes for the spaghetti to cook (usually 10-11 minutes). If you can turn down the heat to minimum and let it gently simmer for a while after this that will help the stock flavour the soup and the spaghetti. Season to taste and then serve.

Minestrone Soup

Minestrone soup is a great one to make as it is so adaptable. You can make a different version depending on what vegetables you have available to put in it so although this is the recipe that the author uses, feel free to adapt it to suit the vegetables that you have to hand, and it also works well as a vegetarian version (no bacon, vegetable stock cube instead of ham).

Ingredients
- Tin of chopped tomatoes
- Tomato puree (few spoonfuls)
- Handful of spaghetti or other dried pasta
- Couple of cloves of garlic chopped
- Bacon cubes (these can be frozen for longer storage but defrost them before use)
- Chopped carrots (fresh, frozen, tinned)
- Ham stock cube
- Bay leaf
- Bit of parmesan cheese if you have it (you can put the left over ends in the freezer for this purpose)
- Some chopped celery (fresh or it freezes well and you can freeze it chopped for easy use)
- Tin of kidney or other beans (drained)
- Dried oregano
- Salt and pepper
- Teaspoon of sugar
- Fresh green vegetable leaves- cabbage or similar chopped finely.
- Tablespoon of olive oil
- Warm water

Instructions

Heat the oil in a pan. Add the bacon pieces and fry until mostly cooked but not browned. Add the garlic, celery and carrots. Cook for a minute or two until the vegetables are beginning to soften. Add the tomato puree and cook for another minute before adding the tinned tomatoes. Stir and allow to simmer gently whilst you add the stock cube to the warm water and add to the pan. Bring to the boil then allow to simmer gently. Add the pasta, bay leaf, oregano, sugar and salt and pepper. If you have a spare bit of parmesan cheese add that too as it gives extra flavour. Add the beans. Allow to simmer gently for 20-30 minutes. Check the taste and add salt or pepper to taste. Put the shredded green leaves into the pot, stir and simmer for another few minutes until they are wilted and cooked. Serve with grated cheese and bread if you have them.

Cheesy Cauliflower Soup

This is a lovely hearty soup that is easy to make and popular with all the author's family. It does work much better if you can blend it before serving though- either with a jug blender or a stick blender works just as well.

Ingredients
- o Frozen or fresh cauliflower (or tinned if you have some)
- o Knob of butter / tablespoon of ghee
- o Packet cheese sauce
- o Milk or milk alternative to make the cheese sauce up with
- o Grated cheese
- o Salt and pepper to taste

Instructions

Cook the cauliflower in boiling water until soft. Fry in the butter / ghee for a moment. Make up the packet cheese sauce and put it into the pan with the cauliflower. Simmer gently for about 20 minutes, seasoning to taste with salt and pepper. Stir some grated cheese through and blend before serving.

Nettle Soup

Nettle soup is surprisingly good! Even the author's children love it so it is well worth a go and as the main ingredient, nettles, are a very easy foraging find, it is a good one to make if you don't want to use too much from your store cupboard. Use rubber or thick gardening gloves to gather the nettles and to separate them from the stems into individual nettle leaves to cook. If you have a blender, this soup is nicer blended. You can put a chopped raw potato or two in this recipe along with the onion if you wish- either instead of or as well as the rice.

Ingredients
- o Plenty of fresh, new nettle leaves
- o Few lumps of frozen spinach, drained tinned spinach or fresh spinach leaves washed (or other green leafy vegetable if you don't have spinach)
- o Boiling water
- o Chicken or vegetable stock cube
- o Some finely chopped onion (fresh or frozen)
- o Couple of tablespoons of dried rice
- o Tablespoon of olive oil
- o Salt and pepper to taste
- o Some cream if you have it

Instructions

Carefully separate the nettle leaves from the stems and wash them. Heat the oil in the pan and gently cook the onion and dried rice until the onion is beginning to soften and the rice is coated with oil- you will need to stir continuously to prevent them sticking to the pan. Add the nettle leaves and continue stirring until the leaves are wilted. Add the boiling water and stock cube and simmer. Once the rice (and potato if using) are cooked, add the spinach and simmer until that is cooked. Blend it and season to taste (or just season to taste if you don't have a blender). Swirl some cream through it and serve with bread if you have it.

Ham and Lentil Soup

This is a fantastic, hearty soup. If you can spare a whole tin of ham then you can make enough to last at least a couple of meals for 2-3 people. As well as tinned ham, this works very well with gammon (if you're doing a gammon keep the water you cook it in as the base for this soup with any leftover gammon bits instead of the tinned ham).

Ingredients

- Tinned ham – cut or shredded into small pieces (don't need much so can save some from a tin used for another meal if needed, or a small tin)
- Dried lentils
- Ham stock
- Hot water
- Bit of cream if you have it
- Salt and pepper to taste
- Carrots (tinned, frozen or fresh)
- Onion (fresh or frozen) and some olive oil to fry with

Instructions

Heat the oil in the pan and fry the onion and dried lentils until the lentils are coated with oil and the onion is beginning to soften. If you are using fresh carrots fry these with the onion and lentils. Add the hot water, stock cube and ham pieces with the carrot if tinned or frozen. Simmer gently for at least 20 – 30 minutes until the lentils are soft. Blend and stir a little cream through if using and season to taste. Serve with bread if you have it.

Main Meals

There are plenty of pasta dishes in this section as pasta is such a good store cupboard ingredient, but a variety of others too.

Tuna Pasta Bake

Ingredients
- o   Tin of tuna
- o   Dried pasta
- o   Tin of chopped tomatoes or jar of tomato pasta sauce
- o   Grated cheese if you have it (frozen is fine)
- o   Some chopped sundried tomatoes if you have them

Instructions

Cook the pasta according to packet instructions (so boil until soft, probably about 10 minutes). Drain and put back in pan. Stir through the tinned tomatoes / tomato pasta sauce and season to taste. Put a third into an oven proof dish and put a layer of flaked tuna on top before adding another third of pasta and the rest of the tuna on top. Add the rest of the pasta on top and cover with grated cheese if using. Put in the oven for 20-25 mins at a medium heat until cheese is melted and bubbling. Serve immediately.

Pesto Pasta

This is popular with all of the author's family and is very quick and easy to make.

Ingredients

- Dried pasta
- Pesto sauce (comes in jars)
- Grated parmesan / cheese if you have it

Instructions

This is ridiculously easy to do and as an additional bonus is a one pot dish. Boil pasta until ready. Drain. Stir pesto sauce (and some grated cheese if using) through it. Grind of pepper on top is nice if wanted and serve with grated cheese if using but nice without too. Any leftovers are good cold as pasta pesto salad.

Lasagne

A selection of different lasagne ideas here. It is a relatively easy dish to make, and works well with all sorts of ingredients so is a good one to have in mind if you have a selection of foods to use. The only key thing is that you need to have the lasagna sheets and it is better with some sort of cheese in it somewhere (whether grated cheese or cheese sauce from a packet). Use the ideas below to give inspiration to create your own!

Vegetarian Lasagne

Ingredients

- Chopped onion
- Chopped clove of garlic
- Tablespoon olive oil
- Dried red lentils (usually a handful or so)
- Tin of chopped tomatoes / red pasta sauce
- Jar of white pasta sauce if you have it or packet cheese or white sauce (can make with long life or soya / plant based milk)
- Tablespoon or so of tomato puree
- Grated cheese (frozen works well for this)
- Extra vegetables such as peppers, courgettes, sundried tomatoes, dried or tinned or fresh mushrooms- whatever you have around- chopped into smallish pieces.
- Oregano, salt and pepper to taste.
- Bay leaf if you have one.
- Lasagne sheets

Instructions

Fry onions, garlic and lentils in the oil until beginning to soften. Add whatever vegetables you want to use and cook, stirring until softened. Add the tomato puree and cook stirring for another minute before adding the tinned tomatoes or tomato pasta sauce. Add the oregano, salt, pepper and bay leaf if using and simmer gently for 20-30 minutes to let it all cook. Preheat the oven to a medium heat.

Heat up the white sauce / make up the cheese sauce. Put a layer of the tomato vegetable sauce in an oven suitable dish, spoon some of the white / cheese sauce over it and then cover with lasagne sheets so there is a layer one sheet thick over the whole of the sauce (you are likely to have to snap bits off the lasagne sheets to make them fit but you can use them in other layers so don't throw them out). Keep layering tomato sauce / white sauce / lasagne sheets until you finish with a layer of lasagne sheets. Cover this with the last of the white sauce and then sprinkle with grated cheese. Put in the oven until the top is golden and bubbling (probably about 20 minutes).

Chicken Lasagne

Ingredients
- o Tin of chicken in white sauce
- o Chopped onions and chopped clove of garlic
- o Tablespoon of olive oil
- o Tinned or frozen vegetables (up to you but peas / carrots / sweetcorn / green beans would all work)
- o Bit of leftover finely chopped ham is nice with this if you happen to have some
- o Lasagne sheets
- o Grated cheese

Instructions

Take the chicken pieces out of the white sauce and chop them into smallish pieces. Make sure you keep the white sauce. Fry the onion and garlic in the oil until beginning to soften then add the chicken. Cook, stirring until everything heated through then turn off the heat while you heat the white sauce in another pan. Layer chicken / vegetable mixture with the white sauce and then lasagna sheets as described in previous recipe. End with white sauce on top of the last lasagna sheet layer and sprinkle with grated cheese before putting into the oven until golden and bubbling. If you don't think you will have enough white sauce, you can add a little milk or milk substitute into it while you heat it up before use to make it go further.

Mince Lasagne

This is the more traditional sort of lasagna, either use normal mince or you can use tinned mince and onions or tinned Bolognese sauce.

Ingredients

- Mince (tinned mince and onions, Bolognese sauce or fresh / defrosted)
- Chopped onion
- Chopped clove of garlic
- Handful of dried red lentils (optional)
- Tablespoon olive oil
- Tomato puree
- Tinned chopped tomatoes or jar of tomato pasta sauce
- White sauce- jar of lasagna sauce, packet sauce or packet cheese sauce (use milk or longlife milk or milk alternatives to make it up)
- Grated cheese

- Lasagne sheets
- Salt and pepper to taste
- Bay leaf and oregano if available

Instructions

Fry the onion and garlic in a pan in the olive oil until beginning to soften. If using fresh / defrosted mince, add to pan with the lentils if using and cook on higher heat stirring continuously until mince is browned, if you are using tinned mince just cook until warmed through. Add the tomato puree and cook, stirring for another minute or so before adding the tinned tomatoes / tomato pasta sauce. Add the seasoning / bay leaf / oregano to taste and allow to simmer gently for about 20 minutes. Make up the white / cheese sauce and warm it through in a pan. As before, layer the tomato meat sauce with white sauce and lasagna sheets, (remove the bay leaf) before finishing off with lasagne sheets, white sauce and some grated cheese on top before cooking in the oven at a medium heat until golden and bubbling.

Putenesca

This is a nice dish to do as it is easy to make, is made from store cupboard ingredients but because of the olives and anchovies has a different flavor so gives a bit of variety. Being pasta, it is filling and hearty.

Ingredients

- Jar or tin of pitted black olives (drained)
- Tin of anchovies
- Dried pasta (spaghetti or pieces)
- Tomato pasta sauce or tinned chopped tomatoes
- Clove of garlic finely chopped

- ○ Grated cheese (optional)
- ○ Salt and pepper to taste
- ○ Tablespoon of olive oil

Instructions

Set the pasta on to boil as per the packet instructions. Fry the garlic gently in the oil until starting to soften. Add the tomato pasta sauce / tinned chopped tomatoes. Simmer gently and season to taste. Once the pasta is cooked, drain and stir in the tomato sauce, and then gently stir through the olives and anchovies. Serve with grated cheese on top if wanted.

Tuna Pasta Salad

A lighter dish so makes a good meal for lunch. All store cupboard ingredients and very easy and quick to make.

Ingredients

- ○ Dried pasta (shapes not spaghetti)
- ○ Tinned tuna (drained)
- ○ Tinned sweetcorn (drained)
- ○ Mayonnaise
- ○ Salt and pepper to taste
- ○ Any other vegetables you have available that you want to put in (chopped peppers, peas etc.)

Instructions

Cook the pasta according to packet instructions and drain and cool. Break up the tuna and mix into the cooled pasta with the sweetcorn and stir in the mayonnaise until it comes to the consistency that you like. Serve immediately or can keep in the fridge for a few hours if you want to make it up in advance.

Corned Beef Hash

A nice hearty dish which is simple to cook. The beetroot will usually turn at least some of the potato pink but that just adds to the charm of the dish. If you have a spare knob of butter, this is nice over it so it melts into the potatoes.

Ingredients
- Tin of corned beef chopped into 1cm cubes
- Jar of sliced beetroot (drained)
- Tinned potatoes (chopped) or mashed potato
- Chopped onion
- Tablespoon of olive oil
- Salt and pepper
- Knob of butter if you have it

Instructions

Fry the onions until softened. Add the potatoes or mashed potato and corned beef. Continue to fry, stirring so the contents brown but don't burn. Once everything is nicely browned, add the beetroot for a minute or two to warm through and season with salt and pepper to taste. Top with a bit of butter to melt over if you have it.

Vegetable Curry

An easy dish to make and possible to do just with store cupboard ingredients but with the flexibility that you can add any fresh vegetables you have too. A meaty version is easy to do- just fry the meat with the onions until browned before going onto the next step.

Ingredients

- Chopped onion
- Handful of dried red lentils
- Tinned or frozen carrots
- Tinned potatoes
- Jar of curry sauce
- Tablespoon of olive oil or ghee
- Rice or flatbreads to serve with

Instructions

Fry the onions and lentils in the oil / ghee until starting to soften. Add the carrots and any other vegetables you want to put in and fry, stirring continuously for another minute before adding the curry sauce. Add the potatoes. Simmer gently for 20-30 minutes. Serve with rice or flatbreads if wanted.

Flatbreads

This is a very basic recipe, but easy to do and a useful one to know if you want to rustle up something bready to serve with a main meal. As well as with curries, it works well as an accompaniment to chilli con carne type dishes. If you have children, they may enjoy helping to make the flatbreads.

Ingredients

- 175g white flour
- 110 ml warm water
- 2 tablespoons of oil
- Oil for frying

Instructions

Combine the flour and oil in a bowl before stirring in the warm water. Mix until it forms a dough and then knead until it becomes elastic and smooth in texture (usually about ten minutes). Divide into four balls then roll each one out flat until it is very thin. Heat the oil in a non-stick frying pan until hot. Fry one flatbread at a time, about 30 seconds a time and serve warm.

Salmon Fishcakes

Something a bit different, which is good as it keeps meals varied rather than everyone getting bored. It takes a little bit of assembly but is still straightforward to do and versatile as it can be served with whatever vegetables you have available. Tinned salmon is usually expensive, but some shops do a large tin for about £2 which makes this dish more affordable.

Ingredients
- o   Tin of salmon (drained and flaked)
- o   Instant mashed potato
- o   Tablespoon or two of breadcrumbs (you can get long life ones) in a plate or saucer
- o   Couple of tablespoons of olive oil
- o   Vegetables to serve with- tinned potatoes / green beans / peas / baked beans etc.- whatever you have available

Instructions

Make up the instant mashed potato so that it is still quite solid and shapeable rather than liquid. Put it into a bowl with the salmon flakes and mix up until you can make round balls with the mixture. Make the balls somewhere between a golf ball and a tennis ball in size. Roll the balls in the plate of breadcrumbs until roughly coated and then gently flatten until an inch or so thick to form the fishcakes. Put the olive oil on a baking tray and put the fishcakes on the baking tray. Cook in a medium oven until golden and the insides are heated through. Check and turn them after approximately ten minutes.

Chilli Con Carne

Chilli Con Carne is a good dish as it is easy to make. It can easily be made as a vegetarian dish, or if making a meat version you can either use mince or other meat such as chopped up sausages for a nice filling meal to serve with rice or flatbread. Make it spicier if you like by adding more spices, and you can top it with grated cheese. Chilli recipes work very well in slow cookers if you have one.

Meat Chilli

Ingredients

- o Chopped Onion
- o Chopped clove of garlic
- o Meat (fresh or defrosted mince, chopped sausage / hotdog / tinned mince and onions)
- o Some dried red lentils if you want to bulk the dish out
- o Tinned beans (traditionally kidney beans but other tinned beans would work too)
- o Tinned chopped tomatoes
- o Tomato puree

- Salt and pepper to taste
- Spices- chilli powder, cayenne pepper
- Mustard if you have it
- Beef stock cube and Worcestershire sauce if you have them (optional)
- Tablespoon of olive oil for frying
- Rice or flatbreads to serve with
- Grated cheese if using
- A little water if needed

Instructions

Fry onion and garlic (and lentils if using) in the oil over medium heat until starting to soften. Increase the heat a little and add the meat- stirring and cooking until browned (hotdog sausages won't brown). Add the tomato puree and stir for a minute before adding the tinned tomatoes. Add the spices and season to taste (you can always add more later). If using, add a teaspoon or so of mustard, the stock cube (crumbled up) and a drop or two of Worcestershire sauce. If it looks like it needs more liquid, add some water and bring to the boil. Once boiling, reduce the heat to a gentle simmer, stir and then leave for 20 minutes. Then add the beans and simmer gently for another 10 minutes at least. You can also put this in a casserole dish and cover and cook at a low temperature (160) in the oven for an hour or more and it will come out beautifully. Check the seasoning and then serve with rice / flatbreads and grated cheese if using.

Vegetarian Chilli

Very similar to the meat chilli recipe above, obviously omit the meat and substitute for plenty of dried red lentils or whatever other lentils you have available.

Add another one or two types of beans for texture, substitute the beef stock cube and Worcestershire sauce for vegetarian alternatives. Use the same cooking method as the meat version.

Pudding Ideas

This section has a few ideas for what could be used to create puddings. You might not want to serve a pudding after every meal, but it is nice to be able to have a few options for special occasions or when you feel family morale is in need of a boost.

Fruit and Custard / Evaporated Milk
A very simple assembly job, but a nice one to be able to rustle up in moments and as it is fruit, healthy too, particularly if we become short of fresh fruit and vegetables.

Ingredients
- Tinned fruit (peaches / fruit cocktail / anything else your family likes)
- Tinned custard or evaporated milk

Instructions
Serve fruit into bowls (either individually or one big one for people to help themselves). Serve with tinned custard (heated) or evaporated milk.

Peach Crumble
This is a little more complicated but worth it as it is a nice filling pudding. Works equally well with tinned or frozen rhubarb or apple.

Ingredients
- o Plain Flour
- o White sugar (ideally caster but granulated fine too)
- o Butter or margarine
- o A few oats if you have them
- o Tinned peaches or whatever other frozen or tinned fruit you have available.
- o Tinned evaporated milk or custard to serve

Instructions

Put the peaches / fruit into an oven proof dish and spread evenly. Sprinkle with sugar. In a different bowl, combine the margarine / butter with the flour and mix. Then add the sugar and mix until a crumbly texture. If you are using oats you can add these in too. Spread the mixture over the fruit and bake in the oven at a medium heat for 20-30 minutes (keeping checking to make sure the top doesn't burn). Take care serving and eating the crumble as the insides do get extremely hot. Serve with tinned custard or evaporated milk.

Tinned syrup / sticky toffee / chocolate puddings

These are a great treat to have in the cupboard! This is an assembly job rather than a proper recipe but they are so nice and handy they are included here for that reason.

Ingredients
- o Tinned puddings
- o Tinned custard or evaporated milk

Instructions

Heat the puddings according to manufacturer instructions. Serve with tinned custard or evaporated milk.

Flapjacks

Another nice thing to be able to rustle up, they are easy to make, filling and sweet so work well as a snack as well as pudding. You could melt chocolate over the top afterwards and allow to set in the fridge if you wanted something a bit different.

Ingredients
- Oats (the same weight as that of the butter and sugar combined)
- Golden syrup (few tablespoons)
- Butter or margarine (equal weight of the sugar)
- Sugar

Instructions:

Put the oats, butter, sugar and golden syrup in a bowl and stir until mixed thoroughly. Lightly grease a baking tin and put the mixture in. Press down so that it is flat and goes right up to all the edges and score with a knife to create the squares / shapes you want the finished flapjacks to be. Bake at a medium / high heat for approximately 15 minutes.

Angel Delight

A great store cupboard dessert which is easy to rustle up. Just follow the manufacturer's instructions using UHT milk if fresh is unavailable.

20- Sample Shopping Lists

This shopping list is a sample to give inspiration in planning your own shopping lists. It is to last a single person 3 days.

- Tea*
- Coffee*
- Box of Cereal
- 2 x Long life milk / milk alternative
- Tin opener!
- 2 tins of soup
- Pack of chocolate biscuits
- Jar of pesto sauce
- 500g of pasta
- Tin of Bolognese sauce
- Tin of Curry
- Packet of rice (for 3 day stockpile you could use a packet of convenience rice that just needs heating up)
- Tin of fruit
- Packet of paracetamol*
- Couple of toilet rolls
- Toothpaste*
- 10 litres of water
- Bottle of wine if you like
- Cigarettes if you smoke
- 3 days' of food for your pet(s)
- Personal hygiene items
- Torch and spare batteries

*Items will last longer than 3 days but if you have them for your 3-day stockpile then you don't need to buy them again when bulking it up to last 7 days.

This shopping list gives:

- 3 Breakfasts of cereal and milk
- 3 lunches :
    - Pasta and pesto (make enough for the main meal to have leftovers for lunch the next day)
    - Soup x 2
- 3 evening meals:
    - Pasta and pesto
    - Bolognese and pasta
    - Curry and rice
- 1 pudding of tinned fruit
- Snacks of chocolate biscuits
- Water

Obviously if you are prepping for more people, you will have to increase quantities and add anything that other family members need such as nappies or baby milk but this list gives a starting point to planning your own shopping lists. The following shopping list is a more detailed version for two people for a week.

Sample Shopping List and Meal Plan for 2 people for 8 days

This shopping list / meal plan was compiled in March 2019, so the prices are current as of March 2019. This selection of food and other products will feed two people for 8 days and cost £40. This includes other essentials such as water, toilet roll and toothpaste. Some items such as the tea and coffee would be likely to last longer than the 8 days.

This is an easy way to either use the list as is to create a quick store to last a couple for just over a week, or adapt to suit your own requirements (for example vegetarians could swap to vegetarian versions of some of the tinned meals). As some of the ingredients will last beyond the 8 days, it will also form a good base to add more to for a longer lasting store. This could be done for not too much extra money.

Many people have asked where to start when stocking up, so this is intended to be a reference to enable them to start quickly even if they haven't yet read the rest of the book.

The majority of the items were purchased from Aldi, with some coming from Tesco. As previously suggested, Aldi is a good place to obtain supplies on a budget, and Tesco also has a good selection of products in its cheaper lines. Some products were on offer when purchased for this meal plan. When compiling this meal plan and list, it was assumed that the cupboards would be reasonably well stocked so it would be likely that there would be butter and salt / pepper if wanted available.

The water used is a mixture of 5 litre and 2 litre bottles. It would be marginally cheaper to just use 2 litre bottles.

Meal Plan

Breakfasts	Lunches	Evening Meals	Desserts	Snacks
Porridge / Cornflakes	Tinned Soup	Tinned Curry, chickpeas and rice	Tinned fruit salad	Pate and crackers
	Instant Macaroni Cheese	Tinned Stew, carrots and potatoes	Rice Pudding and jam	Cheese and crackers
	Tinned Soup	Tinned Bolognese, mushrooms & lentils with Spaghetti	Chocolate biscuit bars (one each)	Pate and crackers
	Leftover Bolognese Bake and Cheese	Tinned Chilli with kidney beans and rice	Peach slices and evaporated milk	Chocolate biscuits
	Baked Beans	Pasta pesto & tinned peas	Rice pudding and jam	Crackers and jam
	Packet Noodles	Tuna Pasta Bake & sweetcorn	Choc biscuit bars	Chocolate biscuits
	Leftover Tuna Pasta Bake	Corned beef hash	Chocolate	Crackers and jam
	Tinned pasta hoops	Meatballs and pasta	Choc biscuit bars	Chocolate biscuits

Plus: 6 x 5litre and 8 x 2 litre bottles of water   £7.96

TOTAL COST   £40.00

Shopping List – Food and Non-Food

Item	Cost	Item	Cost	Item	Cost
Tinned Curry	0.59	Cornflakes	0.50	Tinned fruit salad	0.59
Packet Noodles x 2	0.28	Corned Beef	1.45	Packet Bread mix	0.59
Soap	0.15	Sugar	0.64	Tin tuna	0.89
Tinned Chilli	0.60	Tinned potatoes x 2	0.78	Tinned rice pudding x 2	0.40
Tinned Bolognese	1.50	Pesto jar	0.69	Cheese slices	0.99
Penne Pasta 500g x 2	0.58	2 litres UHT milk x 4	2.20	Pasta bake sauce jar	0.59
Spaghetti	0.20	Crackers	0.40	Baked Beans	0.30
Tinned Stew	1.50	Evaporated milk	0.49	Tinned peaches	0.33
Tinned Kidney Beans	0.30	Instant Coffee	1.59	Tinned soup x 2	0.70
Toothpaste	0.50	Jam	0.28	Jar beetroot	0.45
Tinned chickpeas	0.33	Chocolate biscuits	0.42	Tinned meatballs x 2	1.20
Tea bags	0.85	Tinned sweetcorn	0.39	Tinned peas	0.21
Tinned spaghetti hoops	0.14	Instant Macaroni x 2	1.00	6 pack Toilet Roll	1.99
Oats	0.75	Rice	0.45	Small onion	0.04
Tinned carrots	0.21	Tinned mushrooms	0.41	Tinned lentils	0.55

About the Author

The author lives in a rural part of the UK with their partner and young family. Prepping has been part of their life for a few years, beginning one winter when the local shops couldn't get their deliveries because the roads were shut due to snow, meaning nobody could get out of the village either.

Finding the shops empty of food and with no way to get more was a wake-up call as to how vulnerable our food supplies are. Starting with an emergency supply in case the village was cut off again (which has been used a number of times), the supply has now grown to enough to feed the whole family for a number of months.

Uncertainty over Brexit was enough to justify adding another few months' worth of supplies to the store. Seeing how worried many people who may never have even heard about prepping are about Brexit prompted the author to write this book. The author and family are ordinary people with ordinary jobs and lifestyles and this book aims to show other people what they can do to ensure that their family can still eat after Brexit, giving at least some certainty in uncertain times.